Dating The Enemy

Kaya Potter

Copyright © 2024 by Kaya Potter

All rights reserved.

No portion of this book may be reproduced in any form without written permission from the publisher or author, except as permitted by U.S. copyright law.

Contents

Unbroken - Chapter 1   1

Ready Set Flirt - Chapter 2   4

Charmingly Rude - Chapter 3   6

Daunting Envy - Chapter 4   9

Big or Small; Lies are Lies - chapter 5   13

True Story - Chapter 6   15

Karma's A Bitch - Chapter 7   21

The Perfect Jerk - Chapter 8   27

Dirty Little Secret - Chapter 9   33

Moving Forward - Chapter 10   38

Stomach, Meet Butterflies - Chapter 11   45

Just Let Go - Chapter 12   53

Cupid's Gay [Part One] - Chapter 13   59

Cupid's Still Gay [Part Two] - Chapter 13   64

Jealous Past - Chapter 14   71

I Found You - Chapter 15	78
Chapter	84
Begging You To Stay - Chapter 16	87
I'm Done Pretending - Chapter 17	92
It's Too Late - Chapter 18	98
Chasing Fate - Chasing 19	106
Realising The Truth - Chapter 20	114
Chapter	119
Look After You - Chapter 21	121
My Prince Charming - Chapter 22	127
Graduation Day - Chapter 23	135
Coming Home - Epilogue	142

Unbroken - Chapter 1

Thankyou honey for the beautiful trailer ; its so beautiful :)"Macy..." his low voice whispered, sending shivers down my spine as his hand caressed my cheek. I let the wind blow through my red hair, all while my eyes were shut tight. With him I could forget about my worries - nothing mattered, nothing at all. Just him and me, I let my eyelids flutter open to take in his handsome face, blonde shaggy hair and gorgeous brown eyes.But what I saw was nothing like what I expected. I pushed him away, "Your not Aaron!" I gave him an accisating stare - he simply chuckled, his dark hair nicely styled and piercing blue eyes watching me with a hint of humour. "Your right - I'm not, I'm much better."My eyes flew open, I could feel my heart banging against my cage, heat and sweat prickling my skin. "Blaze..." I let the words leave my mouth, a name to the face. He was in my dream, I had never even talked to the guy before.I shook the puzzling dream from my mind, quickly pushing myself up from the bed. I grabbed the closests items of clothing too me, which turned out to be my skinny jeans and ACDC t shirt. I hobbled down the stairs while attempting to get dress - thanks to that weird dream I was going to be late.I couldn't be late - no way could I be late for my own 2 year anniversary. I passed the picture of Aaron and me posing outside our house. A smile slowly grew on my lips, "I can't believe it's been two years..." And mumbled to myself before I remembered that I was late and rushed out the front door, skateboard in hand, rushing to get to school. ~Arriving at school, I was still pretty excited about Aaron and I's 2 year anniversary. He was the school's star quarterback, smart, caring, funny, incredibly hot and every girl wanted him. I wonder how a skater chick like me got him...I was walking up the steps to the main building when Chloe came running down crashing right into me. She pulled me into a tight hug, "Hey.""Do you mind if we go to the library I've got to print out something before class?" her voice was an octave higher than usual..."Yea, sure but after I see Aaron.""Macy, please come on." Chloe urged.Why was she acting weird...Selena came out next, linking her arm in mine "Come on," she tugged."What's going on?" I raised my eyebrow at them. They knew this was my day why were they trying to ruin it? The very thought was bugging. I shrugged them off, making my way up the steps. Right now i wasnt in the mood for anyone, just Aaron."Sorry Macy," Selena whispered from behind me. What was she sorry for? Then I saw it, Aaron had his arm around some blonde bimbos waist, their lips were locked. She was sucking off his face like there was no tomorrow.I felt my heart, right then shatter into a million pieces... My jaw had dropped to the floor, all I could do was gape at them."You don't need that prick," Chloe quietly said, trying to get me to move. I brushed off her hand, and slowly moved towards Aaron. I stood right in front of him but he was too busy thinking about how many positions he could do her to even notice me."Aaron," I said, but it came out more of a whisper.He slowly turned his head, letting go of the blonde's mouth. His eyes slightly widened in surprise at the sight of me."Ur, hey Mace. Did you get my text message this morning?" Aaron awkwardly shifted. If looks could kill, the boy would be dead on the floor. I gritted my teeth before answering him. "No..." I glared at the blonde girl attached to him, what did she have that I don't? I thought Aaron was the one. That we were going to grow old together, get married, have kids. I was delusional - i finally see he was just another scum."Well, I'm sorry but we're... over," sincerity was the last thing in his voice, the boy i once loved watched me slowly break down. But i refused to let him see me cry."I can see that," I glared at the slut then at Aaron."No hard feelings?" Aaron let go of her waist thrusting his hand in front of me. I glared at him, was he serious? I knocked it away, "Today was our 2 year anniversary."I saw a trace of guiltiness flash in his eyes , "Shit, Mace I didn't mean to..." he shuffled his feet to stand closer to me, I quickly backed away as if he was on fire. I let out a laugh which seemed to startle him, "Oh no hun - Happy two year anniversary - best present ever!" I turned to walk away from him but he grabbed my hand pulling me back."Mace, can we please talk. You dont understand..."I cut him off mid sentence, "Save it for someone who gives a @#^$--" Right when I swore the bell sounded signalling the start of class. I could see people watching and whispering, holding back my tears I tried to hold my head up high."Mace!" I heard Aaron called; I swiveled around on my heels. "Have fun getting STD's TOGETHER!," I shouted back at him. And with that I walked away from him, the only guy who could make me cry, laugh and smile all at the same time. I never wanted to see Aaron again.

Ready Set Flirt - Chapter 2

----> PICTURE OF MACYChapter 2Thank god the bell rang signalling for classes to start, I couldn't take anymore of the staring and whispering. I sunk into my seat in English, I watch as Selena and Chloe sat on either sides of me. Selena put on an apologetic smile, "You sure you're ok? Normal 16 hormone crazed teenage girls don't act this calm."I raised an eyebrow at her, "Are you implying that I'm not normal?"Chloe laughed, "Now you've done it."Ryan sauntered into class, hands deep in his pockets, hair nicely styled. He shot me a cheeky wink - oh how i loved my gay best friend. He sat in front, turning his chair to face us, "Mace, my darling you okay? I heard." He patted my arm sympathetically. I nodded, i bit my lip - lies lies lies! I nearly jumped out of my seat when Chloe squealed and clapped her hands really fast in excitement, "I'vegotabrilliantidea!" she said a little too fast. Selena made a face and mumbled to me, "Here we go...""Well don't you want to hear it?" she asked.Ryan, Selena and me exchanged nervous glances, but Chloe continued on. Chloe was brillant in maths and english - but in her schemes she was just clueless. I was slightly, okay very much afraid to hear her plan."You make him jealous. Once he realizes it was stupid of him to let you go he'll come crawling back to you but you turn him down," Chloe face brightened and she look like she had just achieved world domination. I sunk back in my seat, I did not like where this was going..."And how am I suppose to make him jealous?" I asked in disbelief."You date someone he hates, nuh der." Chloe stated smacking her forehead, as if it was the most obvious idea in the world. Ryan coughed, "One problem genius, no one hates the star of the football team, school captain and the most popular guy in the school.""Oh..." Chloe shrunk down in her seat, wishing to disapear, i nudged her, giving her a hopeful smile. She really was a good friend. "There is one..." Selena interrupted.We all turned to her, "Who?""Blaze Morrison."~~~Blaze wasn't one of the friendliest people in school. He was rude, arrogant, careless but very very hot. He was school's playboy, and very charming if he wanted something. I hadn't had much to do with him, but i know that Aaron loathed Blaze.Chloe squealed again, jumping up and down in her seat. "Excellent, permission to commence plan?"I grunted, which Chloe took the wrong way, "I'll take that as a permission granted."~After another long two periods it was lunch and Ryan, Selena and Chloe couldn't stop babbling about the plan. Selena and Chloe were in deep conversation, heads bent - whispering furiously away. I rolled my eyes before sinking into my seat, poking at my salad with my fork. Ryan noticed my silence, he pulled me in for a side ways hug "You're awfully quiet today, what happened to my ranga firecracker?" he chuckled, i poked my tongue out at him. "Its just..." "I'm not sure I can do this," there was panic in my voice, I hate to admit it but I was nervous."He deserves it, after what he did to you."I nodded, Ryan pulled both sides of my lip into a smile, "There, much better."But my smile faded away when I saw Aaron enter with another girl on his arms, the cafeteria grew silent before an outbreak of whispers spread.I decided to go through with it, nothing was going to stop me.

-------A/N:Sorry its so short.I hope you like it xx

Charmingly Rude - Chapter 3

-----> PICTURE OF BLAZEChapter 3Biology was never my favourite class, dissecting made me faint - more like blood made me squirm. I followed Chloe into biology, grabbing our normal seat at the back. Instead of joining me Chloe ran to Mr Abington and whispered in his ear, he briskily nodded.Chloe grinned and sat down next to me. I raised an eyebrow at her What did you do? And she gave me back an innocent shrug saying Do you always presume I'm up to something. Chloe always had a motive,I had an uneasy feeling it had something to do with the plan. The second bell rang signalling for class to start and Mr Abington was writing something up on the board when Blaze decided to show up for class."Mr Morrison care to tell me why you're late to class?" Mr Abington stood in Blaze's way. Blaze just stood there looking at Mr Abington. Arrogance was just radiating off him, i rolled my eyes as he just stood there. "Well?" Mr Abington asked again.Blaze sighed, "Well if you must know I was doing Sally Cooper behind the shed."The class snickered, they found Blaze's casual sex life amusing but Mr Abington didn't, he started to turn red as a tomato regretting what he had asked, "Take a seat young man." trying to regain authority in his biology class.Class continued normally, the thought going through my head was how was I going to get Blaze involved into this scheme. "Okay class, I'll put you into partners for your upcoming assignment." Mr Abington grabbed his roll chart calling out names to be partnered with a random you could hear moans coming from people as they moved to their new partners."Samson with Taylor, Jillian with Chloe, Ginger with Thomas, Macy with Blaze."I stopped listening to Mr Abington after he said my name, me partnered with Blaze? This wasn't no accident. As I stood up to go sit next to him I saw Chloe pointing and mouthing, "Plan is in action!"I knew Chloe was up to something...I sent her a stoney glare which she pretended not see. I grabbed the work sheets that we were meant to be working on before making my way to Blaze."Hi," I said as I sat down next to Blaze. He barely acknowledged me, a nod was as good as I got. Once everyone had settled down Mr A was going on about some life cycle? I don't know I stopped listening.I turned my attention to Blaze, now how was I going to ask him. I tapped his shoulder gently, "WHAT," he hissed, nearly causing me to fall off my chair. "Ur, hi I'm Macy." I extended my hand towards him but he just rolled his eyes. As if I was a waste of his time. "Your Aaron's girlfriend right?" He smirked, I noticed his eyes would cress when he smirked. "EX-girlfriend." I corrected him. Where had he been all day? The whole school knew by now.Blaze laughed, "What did he do, cheat on you? Turn gay? Personally I'm betting he's a homosexual.""Pfft, gay perhaps but he dumped me today on our 2 year anniversary.""Typical.""Is there a problem, Miss Hawthorne and Mr Morrison? Don't make me regret partnering you guys up." Mr A asked."No, not at all sir." I answered immediately, Chloe would kill me if i stuffed up. "Teacher's pet," Blaze mumbled next to me.Jerk. "So I was wondering..."I didn't get to finish my sentence cause the smart-ass cut me off, "I'm sorry, Molly I don't go out with..." he gave me an up and down glance, "...Your type."I gapped at him with an open mouth, he just simply snorted, "What are you? a goldfish?" I quickly snapped my mouth close. Jerk, stuff the plan.I could almost hear Chloe saying in my mind, "Give up on this plan, and you're letting Aaron win."I rolled my eyes, Jerks these days. "It's Macy, and I wasn't going to ask you out." Well kind of...Blaze's smirk just grew bigger, "Whatever."Another minute of silence, "Blaze?""Hmm?" his voice getting irritated."Hear me out, you and I both know that we don't like Aaron. So I have a plan to get revenge, he hates you right? But he's obsessed with always having the girl. So I say we "FAKE" date to make him jealous. It's a win win situation, you get to make him angry and I get to turn him down. Whadda say?"If that kid had brains, he just made a thinking face. His intense blue eyes were staring straight at me, "What can I say, I love revenge. Babe." with that he winked and went back to scribble on his page.

--Ahaa Blaze is one sexy stud muffin ;)Hope you guys liked it

Daunting Envy - Chapter 4

Chapter 4

The bell rung signaling biology class was over. I picked up my books and was about to leave when someone grabbed my wrist and spun me right round into their chest. I slowly glanced up to see Blaze smirking down at me."So this revenge plan of yours, hows it gonna work?"

"Meet me at second break, at the cafeteria," I said, racking my brain of what the hell I was going to do.

Blaze smirked, "Its a date," before winking and leaving the classroom. I scurried outside before I was cornered by Selena, Chloe and Ryan, Ah my three musketeers.

Selena held tightly on to my left arm, "So how'd it go?"

Ryan was next, "Are you two dating?" he winked.

Chloe was grinning like an idiot; "Am I a genius or am I genius."

I sighed, "Ur, Selena it went awkwardly fine, Ryan I guess we are and Chloe you're a genius. Now can we please get to class, you know Miss Fennel hates me."

~

It was second break, and the cafeteria seemed really far away. I guess this was Show Time and it was now or never. Aaron Ringo Stenson prepare to be revenged on. We slide into our normal red and white booth. Ryan with his daily sparkling water, Chloe and her obsession with gummy bears.

Then in he came, I swear everyone stopped and drooled, it all looked like slow motion to me. Blaze slide himself right next to me placing his arm around me. I pushed his sides scooting away from him, "Heard of personal space buddy?"

"Aren't we dating?" Blaze asked.

"Right," I mumbled looking down, Chloe pushed me back towards him.

"Just to let you know, this is only for revenge. So don't go falling in love with me or anything. Got it?" Blaze voice was edgy.

"Hah! Never in a million years." I stated.

"Blaze this is Chloe, Selena and Ryan."

Blaze did his little guy "sup" nod.

"So, Blaze. Are you prepared to go all the way with this?" Chloe stood triumphantly

Blaze smirked, "All the way."

I made a disgusted face at him, shuffling another few centimeters.

"Well let's get this show on the road, partner." Chloe said in her awful country accent.

Ryan ushered Chloe to shush, which was going to set Chloe on her speech to who knows what...

"Morison, what are you doing here?" a voice came out of nowhere. Oh there standing with yet another girl was my ex-boyfriend, Aaron Stenson.

A frown was plastered on Aaron's face, his eyebrows knotted and his light blue eyes glared at Blaze and me. Blaze chose this time to slide his arm around my waist pulling him closer to him so that I was practically on his lap.

"She isn't yours anymore Stenson, besides waste not want not." Blaze wiggled his finger towards Aaron.

Aaron laughed his eyes showing no happiness, "She's only looking for a rebound guy. You guys won't last a week." It was mine turn to laugh; I turned to brunette hanging off his arm, "Honey, he's cheating on you with that blonde friend of yours." The vulnerable brunette looked up Aaron, "Aarie? Is this true?"

Out of the corner of my eye I saw Ryan and Chloe stifling a laugh while Selena mouthed Aarie? And made a puking face.

"No, baby you're the only on for me," Aaron soothed the brunette as they walked away, Aaron giving Blaze one more death glare.

"Lovely couple, we should totally double date with them, " I joked to Blaze.

"Well, I need payment for dates," he winked at me as his hand lowered down my back. I remember I was in his lap and immediately hopped off.

"Pervert."

"Whatever turns you on." And with that he left.

I turned to see their faces; Selena smiling, Ryan winking and Chloe... Chloe was just happy her plan actually worked this time. "The guy has a massive ego," I frowned at Chloe.

She raised her hands, "Well tough titties, do you want to get revenge on Aaron?"

I nodded, "It's a sacrifice I'm willing to make."

I sighed, revenge was hard work. But it was worth it.

Thankyou for reading xx

Sorry its short i was tireed :)

Big or Small; Lies are Lies - chapter 5

-----> Picture of Chloe

Chapter 5

School was over which was a relief, anymore drama and I'd explode. Selena and me were walking out of maths class when Aaron came over to us. "Excuse us for a minute," Aaron said taking my arm and pulling me away from Selena.

"What," I hissed.

"Stay away from Morrison he's bad news," Aaron's eyes searched mine.

"Hah, that's rich coming from the one who dumped me by text."

"Listen Mace... Macy. I'm so sorry," Aaron pleaded some more.

"You know you never told me why we had a sudden break up. What you do, flip a coin?" I sneered.

"Macy, I felt like we were drifting apart. Besides 2 years was long enough."

"So was I something that you could use until my expiry date came along?" tears threatening to spill from eyes.

"Aww, Macy come one, don't cry," Aaron reached out to pull me into a hug which I avoided.

"Is this manwhore bothering you?" a familiar voice asked.

I looked up through my blurred vision to see black spiky hair, Blaze. I nodded.

Blaze slide his arm around my waist causing my skin to jump, his touch seemed to warm up my body.

I swear I heard Aaron growl at that moment and I had weird scene flash from mean girls. "Come on, Blaze," I said pulling his hand. Aaron stalked away angrily in huff and a puff. Selena saw the dry tears and she quickly enveloped me in a big hug.

"What he do this time?"

"Never mind, I'm fine."

And with that I left both Selena and Blaze, I walked home from school I didn't feel like skating. I need to get some fresh air, my feelings were flying around like crazy.

I opened the front door and I heard mum yell out, "Back so early? Did you have a good day?" she asked, my innocent mom.

"It was interesting," I yelled back before heading towards my bedroom and locking the door. For the first time today I let everything go, the tears stream down my face. I picked up the picture of Aaron and me and tossed against the wall watching as the glass smash into little pieces, just what Aaron did to my heart.

True Story - Chapter 6

A/N:

Heey guys, i posted some photos of the characters. - Sorry if the photos are clear.

Thankyou xx

Chapter 6

A week had passed and the plan was still on. Blaze and I never really talked; it was only for show when Aaron walked past. But what I knew was that Blaze was hooking up with random girls behind the shed, it didn't bother me but hello we were supposed to be dating!

I wonder how long this charade would last, I accidently mention to Chloe that we should call it quits oh boy was I dead meat.

"WHAT? After all my hard work?" Chloe literally looked upset.

"It's just its getting me nowhere."

"But why?" Chloe's eyes were sad.

"Because Blaze's the biggest jerk, after Aaron. And frankly his getting on my nerves."

Chloe looked at me with her puppy dog eyes, "Please... Just hang on for a little longer."

I let out a frustrated grunt before leaving Chloe jumping with excitement over my defeat.

~ Next Morning~

I woke up to an engine coughing out fuel. I looked out the window to see a massive moving truck next door in the driveway. No one had lived in that house for ages, it wasn't haunted or anything just too expensive.

I got ready for school and then skated to school. I collided with someon causing me to fall off and something to land on top of me, "Aye watch where you're going," I yelped. The guy that was on top of me chuckled softly, "Sorry, I guess I'm just attracted to pretty ladies," he then winked with those beautiful green eyes.

I had heard that voice before and I had seen those eyes vaguely before. They belong to Luke Samuels, a mate of Aaron's and of course the schools sleeze. He had a rep of leading girls on for a one night stand than leaving them heartbroken.

Luke treated it as a game, I heard him call it "6 hours to get in and out" I've never really liked him, in fact I never really liked any of Aaron's friends. "Earth to Macy," Luke said waving his hand frantically in front of my face.

I shook my head of the thoughts, "Earth to Luke, you're on top of ME," I pushed him off me getting up, grabbing my skateboard and walking away when someone grabbed my right shoulder, I turned around to see a smiling Luke.

"Hey, so I heard you and Aaron split and now you're with Blaze, you move quick," he said winking, Ulgh Perverted boy.

"Hah that's rich coming from the school's player," I smirked back.

He clutched his chest where his heart was, "Oh I'm hurt."

"Need some ice for that burn?" I asked sweetly.

"The only way you could fix it is by ditching both Aaron and Blaze for me, it'll be a quicky, Promise. And if you want so more you know where to find me," he winked once more before leaving me there standing dumbfounded.

When my mind snapped out of it I turned around and shouted, "PERVERT." He only turned around and mouthed, "You know you want me."

What was it with me and attracting jerks, "Hey babe," said a voice, speaking of jerks. I saw Blaze coming up to me giving me a hug. I grunted after he pulled away, "What were you doing talking to Luke?" Blaze questioned.

"We were talking."

"Hah, Luke doesn't talk," Blaze snickered.

"Well at least his nicer than you," I retorted even though it was a lie.

Blaze seemed amused, "Really... Just be careful around him."

"What's it to you?"

"I don't want to see my baby girl get hurt," of course he had to wink.

"Don't kid yourself," I said before entering school leaving Blaze behind.

It was normal day, me and Blaze met up in the morning then first break and at the end of day, the rest of the day he disappeared. He was probably behind the shed, I shuddered at the disturbing thought.

I waited by my locker for Blaze for a quick goodbye hug I always got on a normal day, but he wasn't there. 5 minutes pasted, then 10, 20. I gave up and started skating home cursing Blaze for making me wait.

When I reached halfway to my house I decided to go through the park so I picked up my skateboard and started walking down a quiet street. I was humming to myself when I heard footsteps, I ignore them this was a busy street it was probably someone walking to their house.

Even so my suspicions were high so I walked slightly faster, praying that I wasn't being stalked. I continued walking, turning into another street another quiet one. The footsteps faded and relief flushed over me, I continued walking until the footsteps started up again.

If I make it back home, I'm making Mom buy me a rape whistle. I sped up walking; the footsteps sped slightly up too. I was afraid to turn around so I kept walking faster until I reached the park. As I stepped on the grass, my feet crunching on all the leaves and sticks, the footsteps behind me did to.

I decided it was time to tell this stalker to back off, I placed my hand into my bag and my hand grabbed my deodorant spray sure it was pepper spray but it was still deadly. And with that I whirled around.

I nearly screamed, but I quickly clamped my hand over my mouth. He was there standing, smirking at me. "All you have to defend yourself with a deodorant spray? I thought you were a more resourceful person..." Blaze said his black hair over his covering his eyes while he could hardly contain his smirk.

"Blaze, what the hell! You scared the crap out of me," I pointed at him.

"Aye, I was just minding my own business," his hands in defence position.

"MORE LIKE STALKING."

"I have better things to do than stalk you, besides just happens were going the same way," he shrugged at me.

"Sure... And where were you this afternoon, I was waiting until school like closed?" I questioned crossing my arms.

"Where do you think I was," Blaze raised an eyebrow at me.

"Ew." I turned and stomped away, thank god Blaze had a brain and dare not follow to closely otherwise he would lose a limb.

After turning out of the park, past 7/11. I continued walking down the street, across the alley, through another street. I could vaguely hear those footsteps. I swivelled around once again, "Okay, you cannot tell me this was a coincidence, I took the long way and you've been following me the whole way."

Blaze had a slushie in his hand, too busy winking at the girls on the opposite side of the road, without turning to face me he simply replied, "I'm not stalking you, trust me."

"Hah that's rich," I turned and walked faster down the road turning into my street. My fake boyfriend's a stalker, GREAT. You know how to pick them Macy.

I didn't know if I should go into my house, in case he stalked me. Or just wait outside, I decided to go into my house, I turned into my driveway, halfway up the stairs when I heard him say, "Oh shit, you have got to be kidding me."

I looked at Blaze who was standing at my driveway, "What now?" I asked. He just stood there looking shocked, "You live here?" he asked, stalker... stalker... STALKER.

"Maybe..."

"Answer the bloody question!" Blaze said getting angry.

"Someone's hormonal. Yea I live here," I regretted that as soon as it left my mouth.

Blaze his hand and pointed next door, to the large house, "I just moved in there."

My mouth dropped in hit the floor, Correction: It didn't hit the floor, it crashed into the floor.

"WHAT?"

Blaze was shocked and pissed too; "Oh Joy!" sarcasm filled his mouth.

We were fake dating and stuff, but in truth we annoyed the hell out of each other.

So he wanted to play the sarcasm game, well two could play, "Well see you tomorrow neighbourunni," I smiled before giving him the finger and entering my house and retreat to my room.

Karma's A Bitch - Chapter 7

Chapter 7

My science homework wasn't going to finish itself so I sat down in my room with multiple books laid open trying to find the answer... If the first consumer is... Frustrated I closed my eyes lying down on the pillow.

I just needed a rest from all this studying, THUD. My eyes fluttered open... I probably imagined it.

I slipped off the bed, wandering around my room. I stopped to look at one of my walls that was painted a pale green. On the wall was about 20 photos of me, Chloe, Selena, Ryan and there was one with Aaron and me, it was our first date, me holding fairy floss and a big teddy while Aaron was looking down at me.

He had taken me to a carnival since he knew I loved rollercoaster's and fairy floss. So he made sure I went on every ride and bought me heaps of fairy floss. At one point Aaron had gotten sick from too many rides but he still went on for my sake... At the end of the day, he played the rifle game and won me a giant teddy bear, clichéd I know but it was sweet.

Now it just seemed disturbing. I walked away, sitting down at my desk turning on the computer when I heard weird noises from next door, Blaze's house. I ignored them at first but the got louder... Was that a groan? Oh EW.

I walked over to my window, and saw Blaze in his room shirtless kissing a brunette chick. They seemed to be going at it. I flung my window open and shouted, "BLAZE!" He was too busy to notice me shouting his name.

I turned my head back inside looking for something to throw, I saw a small bouncy ball and chucked it hard at his window. I saw his head pop up and look around. Once he spotted me he looked crossed, he flung his window open, "WHAT, cant you see I'm busy!"

"Unfortunately I can SEE, so close your blinds and keep the noise down. No one wants to hear your...'business'," I shouted back.

"Hah you're just jealous. Let me remind you, we may be fake dating but doesn't mean I have to be bored to death by you just like Aaron was."

He didn't need to go that far; my heart dropped and tears threatening to return. I sniffled before looking back at Blaze, hurt. "Macy, I didn't mean..." Blaze started but I just waved him off,

"Just please keep the noise down." And with that I shut the windows and my blinds and returned to studying with occasional tears wetting my homework.

~

I arrived at school the next morning tired because someone didn't keep the noise down. I slammed my locker shut turning around to see a cheerful looking Chloe. "GAH!" I shouted in surprise.

"Woah, hey calm down buddy," Chloe laughed.

I yawned, "Someone didn't get a goodnight sleep," Chloe noticed.

"Hah that's because your brilliant plan led to Blaze moving in next door and disturbing my beauty sleep."

Chloe's mouth made an O shape, "Was that sarcasm?" she pretended to be offended.

"No, cause your plans are always fantabulous!"

"Wait... was that sarcasm there?"

"You're so BLONDE!" Chloe looked at me weirdly while pointing at her hair, "Well yeah I am." I rolled my eyes,

We started walking down the hall to our next class.

When Aaron cut us off, another girl hanging off his arms. "Macy, rumour has it Blaze's been cheating on you. This whole relationship with you and him, it's just so planned, so dull. You're doing it to make me jealous," Aaron snickered and so did the girl off his arms.

I sideway glanced at Chloe, I could see her fuming, steam coming out of her ears. Aaron had just call her plan dull. Prepare for hell to freeze over.

Chloe stepped forward poking Aaron hard in the chest, "Don't get ahead of yourself. Blaze and Macy are a perfect couple, so don't dare call them dull. You change girl everyday and they're nothing compared to Mace."

I cheered inside my head, that's why Chloe was my best friend. I looked at Aaron who was a little shock from Chloe's speech but soon recovered.

"Well how come I never see them kiss or spend time together?" he smirked.

Chloe just rolled her eyes grabbed me by the arm, "Oh by the way Aaron, Don't let your mind wander – it's too little to be let out alone."

I laughed at Chloe's remark, "Snap, Sizzle and Burn."

Chloe smiled, "Now to make this plan more convincing, I want to see that ass burn."

~~

Chloe had managed to get a hold of everyone, even Blaze though I was currently not talking to him. I saw out of the corner of my eyes, every few minutes he'd look over an give me an apologetic look which I just ignored.

"Listen up people, Aaron's not convinced so we're going to have to turn it up a notch. Blaze try and contain yourself around other girls. You and Mace have to be lovey dovey, how about you kiss today?" Chloe suggested.

"WHAT?" Blaze and me both shouted at the same time. Selena giggled while Ryan pulled me back down into my seat. Chloe just flicked her blonde hair away, "Come on, its gotta look real."

Blaze just rolled his eyes before saying, "Whatever." And left.

I sank slowly down into my seat, revenge was too hard.

~End of School~

I couldn't be bothered waiting for Blaze at the end of the day, I just wanted to get out of school. But Chloe insisted I wait with her while she cleaned up her locker. I sighed, "Can I go now?" She just shook her head and reached in further.

She was busy chucking out everything from old books, to makeup , to even old lunches. EW. I made a disgusted face as she pulled out a rotten banana, "Cute face," a rather annoying yet familiar voice. I didn't have to turn around to see who it was.

"Blaze, walk home first. I'd rather not walk with you."

Chloe glared at me then Blaze but she also felt the need to step on my foot really hard, it sent the message YOU'RE SUPPOSED TO BE DATING HIM.

"On second thoughts, wait for me Blaze," I said in a fake voice.

"Do I sense tension hear?" asked another familiar voice.

"HEY, that's my line man." Blaze argued.

Aaron just laughed it off. Chloe's smiled wiped of her face, "What tension, the only tension I sense between those two is sexual tension." she snapped back before wiggling her eyebrows at me.

It took all my muscles in my face to not make a disgusted face. Aaron just looked at us, "Sure, Prove it then." I stuttered "I..i... don't think-" I was cut off by warm lips over mine, at first my eyes were open with shock but I remembered to close them and I kissed him back.

Blaze's mouth slightly parted and so did mine; his tongue ran against my bottom lip I shivered with anticipation. I felt Blaze smirk under my lips and he gently pulled away to see confused Aaron. I looked at his face, it...it was hurt... Something inside me wanted to comfort him and tell him this was all fake but then I remembered he broke my heart. I will not feel sorry.

Chloe just smirked at him, "Goodbye Aaron." Aaron turned on his heels and disappeared, I was now faced with a grinning Chloe, "Wow you guys got chemistry!"

I slapped Chloe on the shoulder, pulling Blaze behind me, "Bye Chloe." When we were out of school I turned to him, "Sorry about that."

Blaze leaned down, he was so close our noses touching, I could feel his breath on my cheek, "Nothing to be sorry for." He turned and started walking home. I was glued to my spot, I was shocked. I quickly followed after him, the thing is that kiss was nothing like Aaron's or any other boys, it was special...

I touched my lips, before shaking off the thought and walking home with Blaze.

The Perfect Jerk - Chapter 8

A/N: Hehe so chapter 8. its been awhile since ive updated - so thankyou for waiting. YAY ive reached 1000 reads on this :) Im so grateful, so thank anyone who reads this. CHECK OUT MY AMAZING COVER BTW by Agentcheesecake

Chapter 8

I slammed my room door shut, and fell backwards onto my bed with a big grin on my face. Sure I didn't like Blaze, but I did like his kiss. Ulgh what am I saying, I must be delusional. I turned over, shoving my face into my pillow.

I had a warm feeling over my body; it was spreading like wild fire so I decided to change into short denim jeans and a pink tank top with a frilly hem attached. I hated that tank top that my aunty had gotten me for Christmas but all of my others were in the wash.

I pulled my hair into a ponytail and plugged my iphone into my dock and turned the music to full volume. No one was home and I needed to clear my head from today. Katy Perry blasted from the speakers, my foot started tapping against the wooden board.

After a few seconds my whole body was swinging to the beat, I jumped up onto the bed, lip-syncing to the song through my hair brush. One of bangs fell into my eyes; I blew it out of my face. My foot lost my balance and I went tumbling down onto the floor.

The bang fell in my face again; I blew it away again in annoyance. There was repetitive tapping noise, I got up from the floor, making sure to turn off my music and listen carefully. It came back again, my head turn to look out the window.

I jumped back in surprise to see Blaze tapping on his window with his knuckles; I knotted my eyebrows at him. He simply shrugged than mouthed, "Hold on." I flung the window open to hear what he was going to say but he walked away, What???

I was about to slam the window shut and walk away when I saw Blaze's pure black hair. He was standing pressed against the window holding a sheet of paper with something scribble in permanent marker on it. I blinked a few times, trying to read the words messily scrawled.

Nice dancing... if that was what you were even doing. Oh and by the way you should wear that more often ;)

I choked on what seemed to be nothing but air, he had seen me dancing and me falling on my arse... oh god -.-

I was about to grab a piece of paper of my study desk when I remembered something. I sharply turned my head towards the window again to see Blaze smirking while he was staring at something.

It wasn't my face... something much lower, I remembered his note by the way, you should wear that more often ;) I looked down at me revealing shorts and tank top, and then back at Blaze's jerk of a face. I felt my cheeks felt like they were on fire and my heart beat faster.

I shoved the curtains shut, made a beeline for my bed. Once I reached the comfort of its lacy covers, I snuggled my face deep into the pillow. I drifted off to sleep thinking; Blaze is the only one who can make my heart beat race and my cheeks red… the only one…

~

I woke up to a persistent nagging voice of my 7 yr old sister, Felicity. "Mace! Wake up, Mom says were going for dinner, so get ready."

"Ulgh, in a minute." I closed my eyes again and rolled over. The room fell silent for a few seconds before something cold and sharp began to jab my stomach. My eyes shot open in pain and I glance done at my stomach to see Felicity cheekily poking my stomach.

"Go away Fee," I groaned and shut my eyes again.

I sense that she poked her tongue out at me, "No. You have to get up."

I squeezed my eyes shut, thinking it would make me fall asleep and Felicity go away. "Fee, if you don't go away, I'll tell Martin you like him."

I heard a short gasp, "MOM!" and hurried footsteps scurried out of my room and down the staircase. I relaxed as I was now lying in silence.

It was not too long before a neutral tone that belonged to Mom yell, "MACY! GET READY, WEAR SOMETHING NICE, PREFERABLY GIRL CLOTHES. NO EXCUSES, AND DO GO THREATENING YOUR SISTER, SHE'S ONLY 7…"

"Dibba Dobba," I mumbled to myself, I would get her back later. I pulled my sleepy self up from my bed and walked over to my closet. I flung the doors open, there were skinny jeans, branded t-shirts, shorts, one pink frilly skirt and a dress.

The frilly skirt was supposed to match the pink tank top, i moved away from the skirt. The only other thing in here my mother would approve of was my dark blue dress it had straps that criss-crossed on my back. I sighed as I slipped into my dress.

I quickly straightened my hair, applied mascara on and grabbed my converses and was down the stairs. Mom was waiting by the door in a pretty green shirt and white skirt while Dad had a white shirt on and a plain blue tie on. And little Felicity was wearing a sweet frilly yellow dress; she wore a snarl on her face.

I bent down to her level, "What's wrong grumpy?"

She turned away from me, with a pouted look on her face. I laughed and whispered into her ear, "You look like a princess tonight."

Her face immediately brightened up at the comment, she snuck a look at me then a smile and flung her arms around my shoulders. After a long hug I peeled away her arms, Mom ushered us out the door and onto the driveway.

I headed for the family car when Mom spoke, "Honey, were not driving there."

"We're walking there?" I questioned.

Mom simply nodded and grabbed Felicity's hand, and walked down the driveway. I tailed behind with my Dad, I was glad I wore my converses; I couldn't walk in heels at all.

"You look nice," Dad commented, then he looked down at my shoes and chuckled, "You know your Mom's not going to be too happy with those." I rolled my eyes, "She'll live."

Mom turned into a familiar driveway, she walked up the pathway to the front with Fee tagging along. This house was familiar in every way, because it happened to be our neighbour's house... Blaze's house.

"Uh ah... no way am I stepping on foot in there," I protested, I dug my feet into the ground. "Macy I don't care if I have to drag you inside, we're going to have dinner with the Morison's and YOU'RE going to be polite." I folded my arms and pouted, maybe I could make a run for it.

I swivelled my feet to angle, I swung my whole body in the other direction. My feet were about to take of when I felt two hands grip my shoulders, I looked up to see my Dad giving me an apologetic look, "Mom's orders."

I nodded; I didn't want Mom giving Dad hell. Mom was a very controlling person, but a real lovely person inside. I sulkily stood next to Dad on the front porch, I watched as my Mom pressed the doorbell. A few seconds the door flew open and there standing in the door way was the infamous jerk himself, Blaze.

I watched as multiple emotions flicked by in Blaze's eyes. First surprise, hatred, lust and lastly mischief... Did I just see lust, that cant be right. A smirk started to form on Blaze's lips, "Welcome Mr and Mrs Hawthorne."

Blaze's P.o.V

I stretched out on the lounge and searched for the remote. The news blasted out of the tv stereo, I quickly switched the channel over to a death metal concert. Hmm better. I was comfortable and all when the annoying doorbell rang.

"Mom! Dad!" I shouted from the couch, no one answer. The doorbell sounded again, "Stupid people." I pushed myself up from the couch and walked over to the door, I remember Mom had said we were having people over for dinner. Oh Joy... company.

I swung the door open, I was in no mood to be nice. Standing there on the front porch was a lady with light brown hair wearing a green shirt. She was holding a little girl's hand who shyly peered at me from behind her mother's leg.

A tall, strongly built man stood lazily at the side wearing a blue tie, he nervously looked down at a girl. I'm guessing his daughter. She stepped into full view, my eyes widened in surprise. Macy was the company, FATE's a pain in the ass.

She looked amazingly breathtaking in a dress; it was a deep blue that stopped around her knees. I hadn't seen her once in a dress and she looked beautiful. I felt my heart fasten, and a blush about to form on my cheeks but I shook it away.

While she's here, must as well have some fun... I spread my arms up wide in the air, "Welcome Mr and Mrs Hawthorne!"

Mr Hawthorne firmly shook my hand while Mrs Hawthorne just smiled, "You can call me Lyn and that's my husband Terry. This is my youngest daughter Felicity and my eldest, Macy."

I smiled at felicity and then turned to Macy, "I'm afraid I've already met Macy, she's quite a handful." Her parents laughed and walked inside the house as I watched the pink rise in Macy's cheeks.

While her parents were admiring the room I leaned in right next to her ear, I could her heavy breathing on my cheek as I whispered, "What? No frilly pink dress tonight," I smirked at her embarrassed faced and walked away.

Dirty Little Secret - Chapter 9

A/N; Hah so heres chapter nine. Its raw and uneditted. But i hope you like it :) Ive added some more twists and suprises in.

Chapter 9

Macy P.O.V

I watched as he walked away, as the heat rose on my cheeks. I bet my cheeks were as red as my hair. Blaze had wondered off and so had my parents and Felicity. I sighed and began to take in Blaze's house, pale olive walls and golden tiles. Too my left was the living room which I could see contained brown couches, a fire place and a plasma TV hanging over.

I turned to my right where a staircase was, curious I begin to venture up it. With my hand sliding on the rail I slowly walked while looking at the pictures that hung off the wall. I inched closer to a particular photo with a silver frame that contained a photo with a young girl about 5 years old with her hair in brown piggy tails and a cheeky smile.

She was looking contently up at a younger Blaze, his hair was ruffled and brown he too was grinning down at the little girl with adoration. Blaze looked so happy; I'd never seen him genuinely smile. I continued up the staircase passing more and more pictures. Each picture with different people in it, Blaze seemed to grow taller and older.

After 4 pictures the little girl disappeared from them and Blaze stopped smiling, his hair was now dyed pitch black lastly his eyes showed regret. I stared at the picture for over 5 minutes, It was Blaze standing with a bunch of middle-aged people all smiling at the camera, Blaze was distant.

Something about the photo made chills run up my spine, I shivered in response. I moved away from the photos since I had made it to the second level of the house, the walls were half painted yellow and white with bright lights hanging off the ceiling.

I kept walking past doors, I didn't knowing where I was going but I kept walking until something caught my eye. One of the doors had, KEEP OUT sketched into it with something sharp. I lightly knocked on the door but there was no response so I gently pushed it open.

The room was painted a dark red, there was a bed at the corner with hoodies and skinny jeans messily chucked on top. I'm pretty sure this room was Blaze's due to the poster covered walls, I looked out the window to see it opposite my bedroom.

Yep, definitely Blaze's bedroom. Suddenly the thought hit me; I'm in Blaze's room. I could feel a smile tugging at my lips. He hardly let out any information about him; I began to snoop around the room. I started looking through his bookcase, his closet and his loose sheets of paper.

I sighed in frustration as I found nothing; I collapsed in exhaustion on his bed. I felt my body hit something hard, my hands searched the bed for the hard object I had landed on. I grasped something hard and pulled it out from under the covers triumphantly.

It was a small black cover book, there was a band holding it together with loose papers spilling out the sides. I carefully removed the band. I could feel my heart beating against my chest as I opened the cover. As soon as I opened the cover, the door slammed open and I jumped in surprise, papers spilling everywhere.

An angry looking Blaze stood at the door, arms folded, a scowl across his face. "This isn't the bathroom is it," I squeaked out. Blaze didn't find this amusing especially when he saw what I had in my hands, he rushed towards me, grabbing the book out of my hands and the loose papers.

Blaze sighed in frustration, "What were you doing in here? Can't you read the sign – Keep. Out."

"I got lost?" I avoided his eye contact but I could feel him starring daggers at me.

"Whatever, just get out NOW," he growled.

I quickly ran out of the room and down stairs into the living room, I had never seen Blaze that angry before and I was determined to find out why. All I know is that it has something to do with the piece of paper from Blaze's book that was crammed into my dress pocket.

~

I was seated next to Blaze while opposite was Mum, Dad and Felicity. Mr and Mrs Morrison were seated at the head of the table. Dinner was delicious spaghetti and bolognaise, I kept stuffing food in my mouth while the parents made polite dinner conversation.

My parents seem to be getting along quite well with Blaze's parents. I silently kept eating, shoving more food into my mouth I probably look like I didn't have any manners. Mum looked up and glared at me, Chew with your mouth close, Macy. I could almost hear her think.

I ignored her and kept eating when I felt something warm touch my left thy. I jumped in shock but luckily no one noticed. I looked down at my left thy too see a hand laying on it; my eyes followed the hand up to its arm, till I saw its owner was none other than Blaze.

In disgust I swatted it away, out of the corner of my eye I saw Blaze smirking away. "So Blaze, how do you know our little Macy," my dad spoke.

I choked on the spaghetti that was currently in my mouth and had to drink my whole glass of water. Blaze just smiled and snaked an arm around my shoulder, "Were dating."

I watched in horror as my parent's mouths hit the floor and Felicity started giggling. I was too scared to even see what Blaze's parent's reaction was. I felt something faintly vibrate in my pocket.

I pulled out my phone to see a call coming through. I pushed my chair out and timidly looked at everyone, "Excuse me, I've got to take this," I said pointing to the phone. I am personally going to kill Blaze Morrison .I thought to myself as I walked out into the deck and brought the phone to my ear.

"Hello?" I spoke into the receiver.

"Hey Macy, Its Aaron."

My heart skipped a beat and my eye widened.

"Aaron? Why are you calling?"

"I'm in trouble and well I would've have called the others but their all out partying, but I knew you wouldn't be."

"Gee, thanks for saying I don't get out much. What kind of trouble?"

"My car won't start and I'm deserted in some unknown place, plus I need to talk to you."

He needs to talk to me?

"Let me guess, you want me to come pick you up?"

"Please."

"Fine, I'll trace your call and come get you. In the meantime don't do anything stupid," I grumbled.

"You're the best Macy," Aaron stated before he hung up.

I left the deck and went back into the dining room, "Sorry about this but I have to go, one of my friends is in trouble. It was nice meeting you Mr and Mrs Morrison, thank you for a wonderful dinner," I quickly said before rushing out the front door.

"Macy! Macy!" I heard my name being shouted as I jogged around to my red mustang.

I whirled around, "What?"

Blaze was intently looking down at me, "Whose in trouble?" his expression was actually worried but this all changed when I muttered his name, "Aaron."

Moving Forward - Chapter 10

R ECAP;

"Macy! Macy!" I heard my name being shouted as I jogged around to my red mustang.

I whirled around, "What?"

Blaze was intently looking down at me, "Whose in trouble?" his expression was actually worried but this all changed when I muttered his name, "Aaron."

Chapter 10

"That ass broke your heart and you just drop everything for him," Blake's eyes narrowed.

"He needs help," I protested.

"You're not going."

"You're not the boss of me," I grabbed my car keys from my pocket and placed my hand on the car door.

I felt strong hands push me back against the car, pinning me against the car

"What in the name of-" I started but was cut off by Blaze, "You can't go Mace..."

"Why?"

Blaze looked away, his black hair hiding his blue eyes, "Because... Because you just can't."

I made a buzzer sound, "Wrong answer, just please let me go. Think of it this way its part of the plan. Fool him into thinking I still care about him."

Blaze brought both of his hands to cup my face, forcing me to make eye contact with him, "Do you?"

Now it was my turn to look away, "No," I whispered. Blaze could sense I was hesitating, "Fine, go but I'm coming with you."

I opened my mouth to protest but Blaze had already made his way into the passenger's seat. I sighed and slide into the driver's seat last thing I wanted was a brawl between Blaze and Aaron in a stranded place.

I had traced Aaron's phone call to a deserted parking lot not too far from horse stable. Why in the world would Aaron be there? I thought as I reversed the car out of the driveway.

~

I parked the car on the main road where the street lights shone bright. I got out of the car slamming the door shut, I was glad to get out because the whole way here Blaze wouldn't stop annoying me. First it was the radio station which result in a 20 minute debated argument if Paramore could beat Black Veil Brides in a Battle of the Bands competition.

Secondly Blaze seemed to think he was a GPS, I don't even know why I let him in my car. I began to walk through the field of grass and turned to the path that leads into the deserted parking lot. "Macy! Macy!" a hushed voice called.

"What?" I whirled around. Blaze was jogging to catch up to me, "Were a couple remember."

"So?" I raised an eyebrow. "We've got to act like one," Blaze said as he slipped his hand into mine. I rolled my eyes and dragged him into the parking lot.

The parking lot was completely dead the only light was from the full moon reflecting off the tar. I spotted Aaron's car in the far distances and tugged Blaze's hand for him to hurry up. "Be nice," I whispered to Blaze.

Blaze pretended to look shock, "What are you talking about? I'm always nice."

I snorted, "Don't kid yourself." After another few minutes of walking we reached Aaron's car and 3 metres away there was Aaron half asleep, leaning against the public phones. I cupped my hands around my mouth,

"Aaron!" I called. I watched as he awoke in a daze, a smile lit up his face when he spotted me but then change when he saw my hand was connected with Blaze's.

I quickly rushed over to his side as he tried to get up, "Why'd you bring him?" Aaron growled.

"A thankyou would be nice," I retorted as Aaron gained his balance. Aaron quickly wrapped his arms around my waist and nuzzled his face in my neck, "Thankyou Macy."

I awkwardly patted his back; from behind I could see Blaze with a scowl on his face. I pulled away, "You wanted to talk?" I asked. Aaron smiled at me, "Yea... ALONE," he stretched alone so as if Blaze could hear.

Blaze put his hands up as if surrendering, "Like I want to know about your life-story."

Aaron ushered me behind the public phones, "Listen Macy I know what I did to you was horrible, I can't even imagine what I put you through. I was a BIG Jerk..."

"Yea you were," I interrupted.

Aaron's blue eyes peered down at mine, "Not helping, it's just I can't sleep not having you in my life. I'm not saying we should get back together I just want to be... friends?" Aaron let out a big sigh as he finished.

Part of me wanted to slap him in the face and walk out of his life, part of me wanted to say yes and last part of me well more Chloe said, Remember The Plan... I felt myself genuinely smiling, "I thought you'd never ask."

Aaron laughed as he slung his arm over my shoulder and we walked back to a grumpy looking Blaze.

Blaze raised an eyebrow at our position, "You know she's taken right?"

"Unfortunately," Aaron retorted which made Blaze's jaw clench. I swatted Aaron's arm away and somehow managed to walk in-between Blaze and Aaron.

"Where are you parked?" Aaron asked.

"On the main road, because SOMEONE got us lost at first," I glared at Blaze who had his hands deep into his pocket and grunted, "Not my fault pretty boy got stranded."

I bit my lip to hold back the laughter. Out of the corner of my eye I could see Aaron fuming, his fist clenched. "Hey Mace you look pretty tonight, dressed up to come get me eh?" Aaron relaxed and once again slung his arm around my shoulder.

I was about to answer when Blaze answered for me, "Since when has she ever dressed up for you?"

Aaron smiled and winked at me, "There was this one afternoon when Mace wore her-," I clamped his mouth shut, "Blaze doesn't need to hear about that."

I sighed in relief as Aaron nodded and kept his mouth shut, no need for him to babble my most embarrassing secrets. We were back on the pathway with the mustang just in sight. I was glad this was going to be over soon, I hoped into the car and started the engine.

Blaze was about to slide into the passenger's seat when Aaron knocked him out of the way, slide in and slammed the door right in Blaze's face. I could see how angry Blaze was as he hoped into the backseat. I looked up at the car mirror to see Blaze's normally pale face painted with anger.

Blaze's anger grew when Aaron changed the radio station to Bruno Mars. Aaron started singing along while tapping the drum beats against the dashboard. I laughed and started to join in but every time I looked into the mirror I saw Blaze slouched on the seat with a massive scowl plastered to his face.

I moved the mirror so it was no longer on Blaze's face and returned to singing, this was just like the old time when Aaron and I used to be close.

~

I had dropped Aaron off at his house; he told me he'd find a way to pay me back. Aaron got out of the car and gave me a little wave before going inside his house. When he shut the front door Blaze had jumped into the front seat, staring straight ahead.

His mouth was in a straight line, his fringed cover up his normally lively blue eyes. He was silent. "What's wrong sourpuss?" I purred at him, turning the radio off. "Nothing," he grumbled. "Sure you're not just jealous," I teased.

Blaze folded his arms, "Pfft, why would I be jealous of James Blonde."

"Immature," I said as I turned the car into our street, most households were already asleep, I looked at the clock 10:38.

Blaze look dazzled, "I'm immature? Your the immature one."

"Am Not," i argued.

"Are Too."

"Am not."

"Are Too."

"Not."

"Point proven," Blaze retorted.

I slapped him on the arm in anger, Blaze began rubbing the spot where I hit him, "You hit like a girl."

"That's because I am a girl," I argued back.

"Could have fooled me."

I parked the car in my driveway and watched as Blaze silently got out; I stuck my tongue out at him in frustration. I heard him shout back at me, "I saw that!"

~

I wondered up the steps that lead to my bedroom, kicked off my shoes and laid on my bed. Today had been eventful, too eventful for me. The breeze blowing from the open window sent shivers from my spine. I got up to close it as the wind blew through my hair, howling away.

I pushed the lace curtains to the side, my hands curled around the top of the window. I was about to slam it down when something caught my eye. On Blaze's window was a piece of paper stuck on it and written in pink glow pen was, Immature.

I growled in defeat and slammed the window shut. I stalked over to my bed and sat down in a huff, I swear in the far distance I could hear a deep chuckle.

Stomach, Meet Butterflies - Chapter 11

Chapter 11

CHECK OUT THE MUSIC VIDEO PLEASE ^

Recap;

On Blaze's window was a piece of paper stuck on it and written in pink glow pen was, Immature. I growled in defeat and slammed the window shut. I stalked over to my bed and sat down in a huff, I swear in the far distance I could hear a deep chuckle.

~

I proceed with my normal routine of getting up the next morning, I was halfway through brushing my teeth when I noticed a piece of paper stuck to my cheek.

I detached it from my cheek, running my finger across its smooth surface. I turned it over and began to read the faded writing, It's my fault, she's dead because of me...

I gasped; the paper flew from my hand, now lying on the floor. I quickly grabbed my bag and jacket and dashed out the door, I needed to talk to Blaze.

I ran the whole way to school, my breath caught in my throat, "Blaze?" I shouted when I reached hi locker, he was nowhere to be found, where are you Blaze? "Macy!" I turned around, "Oh Aaron!"

He chuckled softly at my surprise reaction, "Care to have brunch with me, since today is Self-study day, we've got the whole day off." I smiled politely at him, "Loved to stay and chat Aaron, but I've really something to do."

I was about to escape when Aaron grab a hold of my wrist, "Please Macy, lunch by the picnic tables?" he started to pout. "Fine," I admitted in defeat, before checking the remain classrooms for Blaze.

I started walking faster, nearly running and ran straight into a chest. Not just any chest, Luke's chest. "What's with me today?

Attracting all the jerks in my life," I mumbled. Luke's natural smirk grew bigger, it almost couldn't fit his face, "Macy Hawthorne – long time no see."

"And I intend to keep it that way," I retorted and moved aside.

"Oh Macy darling, don't leave yet."

"Well Luke honeybunch, I'm in a hurry," I spat out; I really needed to find Blaze.

I walked away from Luke only to hear him shout, "He's probably by the shed."

I waved in response of a thank you. I walked across the pathway to where the gardener shed was, of course there was Blaze, mouth to mouth with another girl.

I slammed my bag into the shed, causing a ringing sound to echo. Blaze and the girl looked up, Blaze's eyes widened in shock, "Macy..."

I looked away discreetly, "Meet me at the oak tree, whenever your done swapping spit? Kay" I said and stormed off, something inside me was exploding – something I never felt before?

Could it be jealous? I clutched my bag and shook off the thought as I sat down by the oak tree awaiting Blaze.

15 minutes past and I knew Blaze wasn't coming, I gather my things and was about to get up when a shadow formed above me. I looked up and I found myself staring into Blaze's eyes, "What? No more girls to kiss?" I said dryly, for some reason I was really pissed.

Blaze laughed and sat next to me, "Jealous much?"

I rolled my eyes, "Blaze, tell me what happened with your sister..."

Blaze's eyes widened and he refused to look at me or answer me at all. I placed my hand on his shoulder, "Whatever happened with her, it was not your fault."

Blaze started to shake, his voice was small as he whispered, "But it was."

"Tell me what happened," I soothed.

He looked up, he's eyes staring into mine, "What if make a deal..."

I glared at him, "You do something I say and then I'll tell you everything," he offered.

If I knew Blaze – which I did, this was the only he was going to spill. I sigh, "I suppose." He laughed and nudged me, "A date, meet me back here at lunch."

"Su – Wait! I'm having lunch with Aaron," I whispered the last bit, Blaze's eyes narrowed.

"Tonight then, pick you up 6?" he smiled before walking away.

I shouted after him, "Have fun at the shed!"

Blaze turned around and gave me his signature smirk along with a wink, "Ew, too much information!" I laughed and went to find the others.

~

"What do you mean your studying?" I questioned Chloe.

She had her blonde hair tied up in a ponytail, her head bent – reading a study book, "Unlike you Macy, I don't have photographic memory – and I suck at tests."

I sighed and sat down next to her, "Oh well, I'll have no one to tell that I've got two dates today. One with Aaron and the other with Blaze," I smiled as I set the bait.

Chloe slammed her book close, "What?"

"I'm sorry, I thought you were studying?"

Chloe grabbed both of my shoulders, "Spill!"

I told her the whole story, from the start of the day – of course leaving out Blaze's sister.   Chloe squealed in delight, "Make sure Aaron knows about the date and if he somehow finds out where it is, that means he still likes you!"

In Chloe's crazy antics, it kind of made sense. But why was I looking forwards to Blazes date? By the time we finished chatting it was time to go meet Aaron. I found him already waiting at the picnic tables with a box of pizza.

I laughed and sat down next to him, "You sure know how to win a lady's heart," I started munching on the supreme pizza. "This is nice, just like the old times," Aaron shifted closer to me. I just nodded and looked away, "So... what are you doing tonight?" he asked.

I smiled sweetly, "Oh just going on a date with Blaze... You?" Aaron started coughing, as if he had chocked on a piece of pizza. I patted his back to help him; hopefully I wouldn't have to do the Heimlich Manoeuvre. "You okay?" I asked innocently.

Aaron regained his breathing, "Yep, just perfect," he said with a hoarse voice.

~

I walked home by myself today because Blaze had a sports meeting this afternoon, I opened the door and Felicity was running past. And of course Mum was running right past her trying to catch her. I sat down on the lounge and turned the TV on.

"Macy! Don't just sit there, help me catch your sister," Mum yelled from somewhere around the house.

I grudgingly got up and waited by the staircase, Felicity always tried to make her escape up the stairs. I saw Felicity running around the corner, looking back to see where Mum was.

When she wasn't looking I scooped her up, "Hey!" she exclaimed in surprise, I smirked at her, "Gotcha!"

Mum appeared all flustered and exhausted, "Thankyou darling, what did you want for dinner?"

I handed felicity over to Mum, "About that... I'm kind of going on a date," I looked nervously away.

Last time I had brought boys into the conversation, Dad wasn't to happy with Aaron, "Is it that nice boy, Aaron?" Mum asked. I nearly chocked, "No it Blaze, Blaze Morrison."

"Oh the lovely boy next door. Make sure you dress nicely, we should have him over for dinner soon," Mum smiled at me. The front door opened revealing a tired looking man, Dad. "Daddy!" Felicity exclaimed and ran over to him to give him a big hug.

"Macy's got a date tonight!" Felicity told Dad, and then stuck her tongue out at me. Tattletale, I get her back later. Dad didn't exactly warm up to my choice of boys, or any boys at all. If he had a choice I wouldn't have a boyfriend until I was 35.

"Oh really? Name, Age, Address, Criminal record?" Dad raised his eyebrow at me.

I swatted him, "It's with Blaze – the boy next door, you're so embarrassing," I said. I started up the stairs to escape my crazy family, to get ready for my date.

"Honey, what are you going to wear?" Mum asked.

"Skinny jeans and a shirt?"

"Wear a skirt, No skinny jeans!"

I whined, "Why not?"

"Because it's not ladylike."

"Mum, if I can't get skinny jeans off, neither can a rapist – I'm pretty sure safety beats ladylike," I quickly said to shut her up – which it did.

~ 6pm – date with Blaze ^~

Blaze's P.O.V

I rang the doorbell of the Hawthorne's house. The door slowly opened, Mr and Mrs Hawthorne stood there, Mrs H was beaming with joy while Mr H was glaring daggers at me. "Hi, Mr and Mrs Hawthorne, I'm here to take your daughter on a date."

Mr H folded his arms, "Where do you plan on taking her, what time will you be back?"

Mrs H swatted Mr H, "Don't scare the poor kid, just have her home by 11 since it's a school night."

"Yes ma'm and sir," I said politely.

"Blaze?" Macy's voice sounded from inside, she emerged in a superman tshirt and skinny jeans, her hairs was pulled back into a ponytail. "Looking beautiful," I said loud enough so her parents heard, her blush turned red as tomatoes.

As we walked down the driveway I heard Macy's dad shoutout, "Use protection!" I saw Macy turned bright red again, I laughed but then I saw her expression and thought it was better just to keep my mouth shut.

"Where are we going?" Macy asked once I started the car.

"It's a surprise," I was planning to take her to a new café downtown, she'd love it. It has her favourite band, Paramore playing tonight. We reached the café within 10 minutes, I parked the car – I made her shut her eyes as I directed her into the café.

The band was about to get started, I whispered into her ear, "You can open your eyes now," her eyes flew open in awe. She screamed at first then turned around and pulled me into a hug, I awkwardly patted her back, I wasn't good with this mushy stuff.

"Come on, let's get a table."

~

Macy's P.O.V.

Blaze is the sweetest fake boyfriend ever, he brought me here. I was watching him as he gave the waiter our order. When the waiter left, Blaze turned to me, "What are you staring at?" he grumbled.

"You might actually have a heart," I contemplated.

Blaze glared at me, "Jee, what a lovely thing to say to your boyfriend."

I smiled at him; out of the corner of my eye I saw a familiar figure enter the café and head our way, "Oh crap..." I mumbled.

Blaze looked in the direction I was looking and grunted, "Can't I catch a break."

"Well, fancy seeing you guys here..." the figure spoke.

Just Let Go - Chapter 12

A.N; I love writing this story, thankyou so much everyone for supporting me. It means so much to me xx.

Chapter12

Recap;

Blaze glared at me, "Jee, what a lovely thing to say to your boyfriend."

I smiled at him; out of the corner of my eye I saw a familiar figure enter the café and head our way, "Oh crap..."I mumbled.

Blaze looked in the direction I was looking and grunted, "Can't I catch a break."

"Well, fancy seeing you guys here..." the figure spoke.

~

"Oh hey Aaron," I avoided his gaze. Sure Chloe's theory had been right, part of me was overjoyed that he still care, another part was glad that the plan was working. And lastly part of me was sad that he had to interrupt my date with Blaze.

Blaze was glaring straight at him, "What are you doing?" which was a codeword for, Get the hell out of here before I make you. Aaron slide into the chair next to me, "Well I was walking past and there was a new café so I thought and would come check it out!" he said innocently.

"Wait, am I intruding on anything?"

Blaze snarled, "Gosh I don't know Aaron, it's not like we're on a date or anything!" Blaze barked.

Aaron didn't hear Blaze's venomous sarcasm, "Oh that's good then, you won't mind if I join you."

"Yes, we would." Blaze argued.

I sat their quietly, for some reason my voice had vanished every time I tried to speak it wouldn't come out. Blaze kept glaring at me as I sat there in silence, I'm so sorry, I thought to him. Aaron was taping the floor with his Nike's singing along with Paramore.

By the time the food came, Aaron dug in – into Blaze's food. Instead of arguing or even starting fight Blaze got up and left – just like that he was gone. "I thought he would never leave," Aaron said with a mouthful.

I pushed myself up from the chair, finding my voice again, "You know what Aaron, Blaze is kind, caring, sweet, funny and amazing. He also happens to be my boyfriend and we were on a date – so you can get stuffed," I stormed out of the café and away from my favourite band and a jerk-of-an-ex boyfriend.

I saw Blaze sitting on the back of his car gazing up at the stars, his hands behind his head – his expression, calm. "Blaze, please forgive me," I pleaded at his feet. Blaze didn't even look at me, "Only because your pretty," he joked sliding over so I could join him.

I sat next to him studying the stars that shone, "Chloe's going to be so mad," I mused, dreading when I see Chloe tomorrow. Blaze watched me in silence before finally saying, "Why?" I began to count the stars as I replied, "Because I pretty much told Aaron to shove it – which was not her plan."

Blaze doubled over with laughter, "I have never been prouder of you, my little babe is growing up!" he pretended to wipe a fake tear from his face. I rolled my eyes, "I know this hasn't exactly been a date, but will you please tell me what happened with your sister?"

Blaze's blue eyes stared intensely into mine; we ignored the stars and the cars driving past. "At least tell me her name?" I spoke softly. Blaze turned away which broke our stare and returned to stargazing, "Ollie…"

"That's a beautiful name," I really did mean it. "Yeah."

"What was her favourite colour?" I was trying to move into the subject smoothly.

Blaze paused, "Sky blue, like her eyes."

Before I could ask another question Blaze interrupted, "She loved ponies, she hated pink, she always insisted on having rainbow ice-cream yet always end up swapping for my chocolate mint. She loved to dance and sing and was always practicing in her room, blasting her music so the whole neighbourhood could hear, she was cheerful, bubbly, enchanting and kind."

I placed my hand on Blaze's arm, "I wish I could have met her."

Blaze let out a weak chuckle, "She would have loved you, she always wanted an older sister – and insisted she would be my "Best Man" or in her case, Best Sister."

Blaze continued, "But then it all went wrong, her 10th birthday party was at a farm in the country and we had drove all her friend there for singing, dancing and of course pony rides. When the food was ready I went to call all the kids in, I saw Ollie in her blue overalls running to catch her pony, Sky who had gotten lose. The next thing I knew she was on the main road and the car didn't see her…" Blaze had his head in his hands; I could hear small whimpers escaping his lips.

I pulled him into a hug, his head resting on my shoulder I could feel tears seeping into my shirt; I had never seen Blaze this vulnerable. "It was my entire fault, I should've jumped in front of the car or pulled her back or something…but I didn't," he whispered into my neck.

"It wasn't your fault Blaze, you couldn't have saved her and she wouldn't want you to hold yourself responsible." I soothed.

"I know but I'm her big brother, I'm supposed to protect her – always."

"It's going to be hard, but you've got to let her go Blaze."

"I know – I've tried before but it's impossible," he let out a big sigh.

"But now you've got me to help."

Blaze looked at me with his red eyes, "Thank you."

I leaned in closer and pressed my lips against his cheek, I whispered, "I'm here for you."

I pulled away to see Blaze's usual cheekiness returned to his face, "I believe my lips are over here," he pointed to his lips.

"I'm sorry I don't kiss fish lips," I teased and jumped off the back of the car.

Blaze laughed, "Then what do you call Aaron's?" we both started laughing.

I poked my tongue out at him, "You're just jealous that you're not going to get a kiss from me," I teased.

With a smooth movement Blaze was only arm's length away, "Not if I can help it," he spoke in a low, creepy voice. I quickly dodged his little "hug" attack and ran away squealing, "Pervert!"

Blaze waggled his eyebrows, "You know you love it," that's when he scooped me up in his arms, my nose was touching his – maybe we were just to close. If we had stayed like this for any longer we would have kissed but we didn't because my phone chose that exact moment to ring.

Blaze gently put me down; my feet hit the gravel, "Hello?"

A muffled voice spoke, "IS HE THERE?" it screamed…

"Chloe?" I made out the voice, Blaze raised an eyebrow at me.

"Tell me all the details, did Aaron storm in? What did Blaze do?"

"Chloe don't get angry but I kind of told Aaron to shove it," I nervously laughed.

"YOU WHAT?" Chloe shouted through the phone.

"Chloe come on, he was being a jerk!"

"My precious plan – ruined…" Chloe went silent.

"Chloe? You still there?"

"Wait, I could work with this – I could make this work!" Chloe squealed with delight, I could hear her sketching away on paper. I sighed, "Goodbye Chloe," I hung up before she could explain further.

Blaze was suppressing a laugh; I swatted him, "Not funny, I'm worried. Knowing Chloe she's going to make this plan even more extreme than the last one."

Blaze let out a loud laugh, "As long as there's kissing I'm fine,' he opened the car door for me.

"That's why I'm worried," I joked and slid into the car.

Cupid's Gay [Part One] - Chapter 13

A/N; Ooohhh, im loving the idea i got ! Its going to be soo cute. So this is the short bit of a very long chapter. Its split into two, the second part will be updated soon i promise !

Anyways enjoy xx

Chapter 13 - Part One

"I'm thinking big hearts and pink ribbons, Oh and CUPID!" Chloe clasped her hands together excitedly as Blaze and I slumped in our chairs in the cafeteria. She twirled her blonde hair within her manicured fingers, "How romantic," she sighed dreamily.

Ryan and Selena were nodding along, their eyes shinning with their love for the holiday. I used to like Valentines Day, back when i had a real boyfriend and he'd surprise me with chocolates and flowers and teddys. I took a glance at Blaze, no way would this one be caught in flower shop, let alone buy any.

"Oh and of course there is the Valentine's day Dance this Saturday – matching outfits!" Chloe squealed, the girl was more perkier than barbie's plastic boobs. She giggled jumping up and down, her hair wildly following

I banged my head against the table groaning, Blaze was doing the exact same. "I'll be cupid!" Ryan winked at me, before winking at Blaze - a little too long for my liking. I laughed as Blaze squirmed uncomrfortably. "You sure Ryan?"

"Oh yes! I've got the costume and everything!" he exclaimed, i let out a snort imagining him in a big diaper and wings.

"Chloe.. say you dont have another idea?" I cringed as the picture of her with a bunch of pink stuff popped into my head. Knowing Chloe, she had a new scheme everyday.

Chloe leaned in, making us all huddled stupidly, "Well were going to make the whole school jealous by making everyone think that Blaze is the most romantic and amazing guy in school. And since the Valentine's day Dance Couple of the Year Comp is on – that Aaron always wins, Blaze is going to win!"

I burst out laughing, "Him? The most romantic man in school – your kidding!"

Blaze looked taken back, "What are you implying?"

"I bet you don't even know when Valentine's Day is," I smirked. The guy probably only knew what the 14th of february was because he got easy shags from single girls. I raised a brow at him, challenging his knowledge

"Oh you're on... Be prepared to be loved out," he snarled and stomped off, shaking his head.

Chloe raised an eyebrow at me, "Weirdest argument ever..."

~

It was finally Valentine's Day, I had hardly seen or heard from Blaze the whole entire week, im expecting him to keep a down low, since its the "big day!" as Chloe liked to call it. As i skated past Blaze's house, my hands were empty - no valentines present for him. But what would he want?

Racking my mind, i turned the corner. What would someone like Blaze want? I bit my lip, there was no way i was getting him a condom. I bent down slightly, roudning the curb as i pluck a flower from Mrs Hopton's garden. This will do Blaze, its the thought that counts... right?

Chloe was waiting for me on the wooden bench outside school, an enormous bag next to her. "What's in there?" I asked warily, as i picked up my skateboard. Big suprises and Chloe just dont mix.

"Your dress for tomorrow." I swallowed loudly, following Chloe as she made her way into school. I quickly shoved the bag and my skateboard into my locker,and slammed it shut. I honestly dont think i have mental stabllity to dare open it.

I let out a scream as Blaze's face pops up from behind me, my hand flew to my mouth as i tried to stop myself from hyperventalating

"You scared me," I stated.

Blaze smirked, "Oh it gets worse..."

My eyes widened in confusion, I watched as Blaze signalled to a group of boys, some wearing red hearts, lip stick smudge on their cheeks. Two of them even had a guitar, one with a tambourine. Oh no... I turned to Chloe, "Did you set this up?" i mouthed.

She shook her head, she was clearly in shock too. I turned back to them as Blaze mummbled a clear, "1, 2, 3."

"Baby you light up my world like nobody else, the way that you flip your hair gets me overwhelmed. The way you smile at the groound it aint hard to tellllllllll! You dont knoooooowwwww, you dont know your beautiful. Oh oh! That's what makes you beautiful!" Blaze and his boy band sung, a crowd had started to forming as Blaze continue to serenade me.

My eyes were now size of saucepans, i didnt know whether to be horrified or flattered. Horrified that Blaze even knew a One Direction song, flattered that he tried to sing it. More people started to stare as Blaze took my hands twirling me along with him.

I tried to cover my face with my shoulder but Blaze refused, the big idiot was making a scene just to prove a stupid bet. The next minute he's hollering down the halls for a cupid, what in the world...

"CUPID!" he called out again.

Okay.

This is probably the most disturbing thing ever, Ryan in a diaper with fairy wings including the bow and arrow. I let out a snort as Ryan gracefully walked over to us as he shot heart arrows at people Which caused them to gawk some more, their heads nearly blew up when the saw Blaze pull out a bouquet of red rosees.

"Be my Juliet, the dance tomorrow night?" he announced loud enough for everyone to hear. He shot me a dirty smirk as everyone gasped. Everything was going as he planned, he was probably going to get a lot of numbers after this.

I blushed bright red and nodded as Blaze scooped me into a tight hug and whispered into my ear, "Aaron saw the whole thing – the bait is set. And you said I couldn't be romantic..."

"Yeah yeah, Romeo," i grabbed his bouquet slapping his shoudler with it. I joined Chloe, linking arms with her. Not before turning back to see a crowd forming Blaze, who was look straight at me, "Happy Valentines Day," he mouthed before turning to a short blonde.

I smiled, maybe today wasnt too much of a 'facade'

Cupid's Still Gay [Part Two] - Chapter 13

C
HAPTER 13 PART TWO

HAPPY VALENTINES DAY !

"Wow Macy you are so lucky to have Blaze," a girl from my Spanish class mummered to me as i passed her in the hall.

I smiled politely, "Thanks."

All day I've been getting praise from others, everyone whispers when I walk past – they've also started glaring at Aaron and well no one can look at Ryan without laughing. I raised my eyebrow at Ryan as we walked to our next class, "It's not my fault I made a sexy cupid," he flashed me a cheeky smile.

I swatted him, "A grown man a diaper is not sexy."

"For gay men it is," he said before flicking his hair, i gave him a deadpanned look, "WAY! too much information."

~

I glared at the dress sprawled on my bed, it was a sleeveless dress that would stop at my knees – made of pink silk covered by delicate black lace. I didnt expect Chloe to pick a dress like this, i something expected more frilly...

It was beautiful - simple but yet elegeant but I didn'teven know how I was going to pull it off - I glanced at my reflection, i looked like a had just woken up from a 100 year slumber. My hair was messily standing up in different directions. My eyes seem to have darkened with eyebags and my chaped lips looked unfixable.

As if on cue Chloe and Selena waltzed into my room, Selena carrying boxes of makeup, a whole crate of it. I cringed at the site, they know i hate anything unnatural, and Chloe wasnt gentle at all when it came to applying makeup.

I remember that time she poked a mascara brush into my eyeball, i shuddered. Was it too late to back out? As if hearing my thoughts, Chloe moved in, she flashed me a toothy grin "Make over time..."

~ An hour of pure pain later~

"I didn't know waxing could hurt that much," I examined my poor legs in the mirror, the stinging sensation just wouldn't go away. I could see Chloe examining me through the reflection. She smirked, "Pain is beauty – by the way what shoes are you going to wear?"

I smoothed my dress down, "Um vans?" I squeaked flashing her a nervous smile, no way could i walk in anything high, especially after Chloe's leg torture. Chloe narrowed her eyes and tossed a pair of black stilettos at me, "These will do," she tottered to the bathroom carrinng her dress.

I turned to Selena who was suppressing a laugh, "If i were you, id wear them."

I put them on hesitantly, "So evil," I said flatly as I tried to balance before i knew it, i began to lean to one side before i crumpled to the ground.

Chloe emerged in a pretty blue dress that framed her delicate figure perfectly; her blonde hair was twirled into complicated looking bun. I turned to see Selena in a red dress that sparkled every time she moved – they both looked stunning. I enveloped them in a hug, it was moments like these that i remember im so lucky to have them, "I love you guys," as i pulled them into a hug.

Chloe pulled away first, "Now dont get all teary, dont want you ruining your makeup."

I looked at myself in the mirror; my red hair curled, my shiny lips, flawless makeup, a beautiful dress and my awkward legs shaking in the high heels. I felt myself smile, I thought I looked pretty – and I hoped Blaze would to.

~

"Aww look at the cute couple!" Mum gushed as she made me and Blaze pose for a photo. the 100th photo. My jaw hurt from smiling, my feet were already aching. "Mum! This is not prom," I whined as Chloe, Selena and Ryan joined in the picture, they were all smiling like crazy, except Dad and me.

Dad wasn't too happy with Blaze's arm around my waist, he would pretend to have a coughing fit whenever he thought Blaze got too close to me. I watched as me Dad choked, "Too close," he mummbled before covering it up with another cough.

"Think your coming down with something, Mr Hawthorne!" Blaze smirked, as he tightened his grip around my waist. Dad's face went red, his eyes nearly popping out of his sockets. I rolled my eyes as Blaze pulled me into a hug as mum snapped away like she was the paparazzi.

I whispered to Blaze as I put on a fake smile, "Can we please go?"

Blaze looked down at me, his sea blue eyes cause the world around me to fade away, "Anything for you princess," he purred as he let go of my hand to talk to my mother and father.

Leaving me swooning, few minutes later I was in Blaze's car on the way to school, "What did you do to convince my mum to stop taking pictures and dad to let me into your car without attaching a tracking device?"

Blaze gave me the weirdest look, "They just couldn't resist my natural good looks and charm," he winked and pulled over into the next lane. I snorted, "How many times have I heard that lie – I'm surprised your nose isn't like Pinocchio," I teased.

Blaze laughed sarcastically, "You're so hilarious." he flashed me a deadpanned look before turning back to the road, " You know Chloe's right on our tail."

I looked into the side mirror to see Chloe's convertible revving behind us, you could notice the girl's driving anywhere. Chloe's driving was way more dangerous than her schemes. "Satan's spawn…" I muttered to myself.

Blaze choked on thin air, "And you're not?"

I snorted once again, "You're such a hypocrite."

Blaze pressed the horn at the car in front of us, "You're starting to sound like a pig, with all that snorting."

I slapped his arm, "At least I don't eat like one."

Blaze pulled into the street that lead to the school, "I eat perfectly normal."

"Chew any louder and nosier people will start thinking Godzilla's arrived," I over exaggerated as i pretended to chomp the air.

Blaze just rolled his eyes, "Lame."

I watched as he turned into the school driveway, I could hear the music pumping through the hall travelling down the road. I smiled as cars started to arrive from every direction. It was time to put Aaron in his place, to show him i didnt need him anymore. I wasnt just some game.

I swung the door open, pushing Blaze's hand away. He's put on his prince charming act again, my stilettos hit the floor, next thing i began to slant. If Blaze wasn't standing there I would have fallen over, "Not so graceful now are we Cinderella?" I pushed past him walking confidently to join Chloe, Ryan and Selena.

~

We entered the hall which had been transformed into nightclub pretty much. Disco balls, a DJ, coloured lights and energetic people dancing. I looped my arm around Blaze's as he did the same, we were halfway down the steps when a spotlight flashed into my eyes.

I put my arm to cover my arms as Blaze muttered, "What the hell?" the light stung my ears, i rapidly blinked, clutching tighter to Blaze - afraid of missing a step and tumbling over.

"My fellow students and chaperons, introducing our Cinderella and Prince Charming, Our Romeo and Juliet. Mulan and General Shang - Our Blaze and Macy!" Chloe's voice boomed from the speakers, I saw heads turn and stare at us.

I groaned, the girl just doesnt stop. "Did she just refer us to a disney asian couple?" Blaze mumbled to me. I cringed, "Yes, im afraid she did." The intense spotlight gave us no hope of disappearing.

I glanced into the sea of faces, some showed awe, some jealously. And one specific face, filled with anger and hatred - Aaron's. Blaze put on a smile, tugging me closer "Here that – at least someone thinks im Romeo material," as he dragged me onto the dance floor.

I laughed as Blaze was attempting to dance with me, he spun me around enthusiastically - as if to mock everyone else. The guy was such a pooper. He later excused himself to mingle with others. I knew he was going to hook up with some random girl.

Not letting that get to me, i continued dancing with Ryan and Selena, i let my head lean on their shoulders as i smiled. This is probably the happiness ive ever been. I glanced up to see Chloe bossing the DJ around, I shook my head with laughter – she's one scary lady.

My laughter soon stopped as i spotted Aaron making his way through the crowd. His eyes straight at me, i could feel my palms begin to sweat and my heart beat faster.

He suddenly stopped, a sadness expression flashed across his face. He looked away, blue eyes clouding up before he stalked away, hands shoved deep into his pockets.

I crinkled my forehead together, what just happened? I turned around to see what scared him away, where his gaze had been. And there was Blaze holding a corsage, it was beautiful, its delicate white petals decorated with peachy swirls.

I watched in awe as he slipped it onto my wrist, "You look beautiful tonight!" i could feel my cheeks slowly heating up.

"Aw thank you, you're looking handsome to," I smiled at the compliment, thank goodness it was too dark to see my blush. Blaze laughed, "Why wouldn't I."

The music faded away as Chloe took to the stage with an envelope in her hand, "Thanks to your votes, it's time to announce the Valentine's Day Couple... Is..."

Chloe loves suspense; unfortunately she never got to announce the winners since a girl in combat boots swiped the microphone from Chloe, "Blaze Henry Morrison! You have some explaining to do!" her blonde hair glowing from the spotlight.

Chloe was gawking at the scene in front her, she absolutely hate it when her spotlight is stolen. I watched as they began to bicker, Chloe gesturing to Blaze and me, i turned to Blaze.

I felt him stiffen next to me, "Oh crap."

dramatic music :L i love cliffhangers, so what do you think will happen next? predictable - or not? Anyho thankyou for supporting me^ Ive reached 200 fans and 20 000 reads. (:

Hope you liked this chapter, the dress MAcy wears is on the side, its beautiful ^^ Annd im thinking of writing a sequel to this story? Do you guys think i should;;

Oh and any title suggestion?

Love^

Eunice

Jealous Past - Chapter 14

----- > Lucy !!

Chapter 14.

I looked at Blaze as his hands were now balled into fists and a scowl had replaced his smile. "What's wrong?" I whispered to him, tugging on his sleeve. He pushed me behind him – like he was protecting me, somehow.

The girl marched down, almost like a showdown. Her arms were crossed as her eyes glared at Blaze and me. Her blonde hair matched her pale complexion, her brown eyes, cold and demeaning. She was beautiful! "Lucy," Blaze spat out.

Lucy continued to glare at me, I gulped. Blaze gripped my hand reassuring me that it would be okay – who was this girl, a physcopathic ex? "Who is she?" I whispered into Blaze's ear. Blaze leaned back and whispered "No one."

Lucy had obviously heard because her eyes had widened, her mouth forming an O shape, "NO ONE! I AM NOT NO ONE- I AM HIS GIRLFRIEND!" she screamed, a crowd had started to form.

My eyes searched the crowd for Chloe; I could see her up on the stage talking to people who look like security. She was ruining her hand through her hair in panic, why is she panicking! shes not the one whose caught in a lovers fued. I turned my attention back to Blaze. "EX!" Lucy turned her gaze to me, "You boyfriend stealer – he's mine you hear me!"

I backed away, Blaze took a few steps to her – then grabbed her wrist before dragging her towards the outside gardens. Lucy was yelling quite violently too, Blaze's expression had turned serious as he continued to drag her outside. i could hear Lucy's screams had slowly faded, I realized the crowd was all watching me – expecting some fight or breakdown. My cheeks were turning red, all their stares burning holes into me.

"Nothing to look here people!" a voice I've known to love and hate.

"Aaron?" I looked as he shooed people away, the music started again and everything return to normal.He pulled me into a warm embrace as he started to sway to the music, "What are you doing?" I muttered into his warm chest.

"Shh, just one dance," he wrapped his arms around my waist and pulled me closer to him. I breathe in his familiar, intoxicating scent, "Just one dance," I whispered to him as I closed my eyes and relax.

Blaze's P.O.V.

Lucy continued screaming even though we were far away from the hall, I rolled my eyes she had always been a drama queen. I suddenly stopped, letting her wrist go as she stumbled to a halt. "And you said I couldn't act!" Lucy stuck her tongue out at me.

I laughed, "It was a good performance I must admit – you act like all my ex-girlfriends," I stretched my arms as I let out a yawn. Lucy just shook her head, her blonde curls going wild, "Don't let that get to your head, and remember the original plan."

I nodded, I had asked Lucy – my best friend since forever to pretend to be a stalker of an ex-girlfriend to see how Macy would react and if she got jealous that means she cares. The reason why I had gone to such drastic actions was because what Chloe had told me the other day was driving me crazy.

Flashback

"Blaze!" I turned around just in time to see Chloe rushing towards me.

"Sup?"

"There's something I need to tell you…"

"Tell me what?" I questioned what she was talking about.

"It's a secret so don't tell anyone," Chloe was frantically looking around.

I rolled my eyes and mocked her, "Cross my heart and hope to die."

Chloe nodded and whispered into my ear, "Macy likes you – for real."

I nearly choked as Chloe pulled away and gave me a stare that said "Don't tell anyone!"

I nodded – ever since then, it replayed in my mine. Did she really like me?

end of flashback

"Do you like her?" Lucy's soft voice brought me back to reality.

I coughed, "No?"

"You said that like a question."

"You're hearing things."

"You like her – don't you," Lucy teased. "My little Blazey boy is in love!"

I pouted and folded my arms like a stubborn little boy, "Am not!"

Lucy laughed and pinched my cheek, "Blaze and Macy sitting in the tree, K-I-S-S-I-N-G…"

"Stop it!" I swatted her hand away from my now sore cheek.

"Blaze?" Chloe's voice came from around the corner.

Lucy and I immediately froze; Chloe came around the corner – eyebrow raised.

"What's going on here?" she asked.

I quickly moved away from Lucy, "I was telling Lucy that she can't just make a scene - were broken up, finished, done."

Lucy quickly recovered and went back into acting mode, "But Blaze… I love you!"

I dodged her attempt of a hug, "Where's Macy?" finally realizing I hadn't seen her since Lucy dropped by.

Chloe's eyes avoided my gaze, "Chloe? What's going on?"

"She's umm kind of, with… Aaron," she stuttered.

"What do you mean, kind of with Aaron?"

"She's dancing with him – she hasn't left his side since you disappeared."

I pushed past her back into the hall, they were playing Party Rock Anthem, lights were flashing – people were getting close to each other. I spotted her fiery red hair; her head was resting against Aaron. I watched as Aaron began to slide his hand further and further down until it rested near Macy's butt.

I pushed towards them, dodging sweaty people. I threw Macy from his embrace, "What the hell is happening here?" I barked. Aaron regained his balance and squared up against me. "I was just giving your girlfriend the night she deserves," he spat back.

"What? By feeling her up!" I glared at him.

"What about you? Dragging your secret lover off!" Aaron shot back.

I grabbed Aaron's collar, "That's none of your business – she is MY girlfriend not yours," I snarled at him, I felt tiny hands pulling my arm off Aaron, "Blaze, please stop!" Macy's voice cried.

I looked into her pleading eyes and after a few minutes of hesitation I let go. "I'm out of here," I muttered and pulled my arm away and walked out the front doors.

Macy's P.O.V

I watched as Blaze stomped out of the hall leaving me all alone. What had happened, I promise Aaron just one dance which had turned into past feelings and lust. I shudder at thought, Chloe would not be happy. Speaking of Chloe where was she?

"Macy, why are you with him?" Aaron mumbled into my hair. I felt comfortable there but it felt wrong almost like I was betraying Blaze. I pushed myself away, "No – I can't do this Aaron." I searched the crowd, spotting Chloe's blonde head bobbing in and out of the crowds.

I finally managed to find her, "Chloe!"

"Macy!"

"Do you know where Blaze went?" I asked.

She shook her head, "What happened with you and Aaron?"

I could feel my face heating up with embarrassment, "Nothing... just nothing..." I stuttered.

Chloe raised an eyebrow at me, she knew I was lying but she didn't press any further. She tugged at my arm, "This party sucks, let's just go," she pulled me away from the hall. I was grateful to have her as my best friend but I couldn't help feel she was hiding something from me.

"Do you know the girl with the blonde hair?" Chloe asked.

"Who?"

"The girl who was screaming at Blaze..." Chloe searched my eyes for answers.

I could feel my blood boiling at the mention of her; I still didn't know who she was just that she was an ex-girlfriend of Blaze's. "An ex-girlfriend," I muttered to myself, I wrapped my arms around myself as the wind bit against my skin.

Chloe nodded, she muttered something under her breath that I wasn't suppose to hear, "Well it looks like something more." I bit my lip as I made my way to Chloe's car – it wasn't until I tasted the salty liquid that I noticed that my lip was bleeding.

A/N; Thankyou guys for all the support you've given me. Im sorry i've been an evil little munchkin and havent uploaded i've been busy with exams.

But since its winterbreak! ill try and upload quicker (: Im so happy i've 293 fans. Im hoping to reach 300 ? yeah thats my goal.

Anyho, thanks guys.

Love, Laugh, Live.

xx

I Found You - Chapter 15

Chapter 15

Mrs Morrison P.O.V

"That must be her," I muttered to my husband as I glance around the room making sure everything was perfect. None of Blaze's boxers lying in site, i let out a sign of relief before dusting my hands on my back of my jeans. I opened the front door; flashing Macy a wide grin "Welcome Macy, make yourself at home!"

She gave me a small smile, her eyes searching around the room. "Hello Mrs Morrison – I'm just wondering what's going on? I got a text from my Mum saying to grab some clothes and come over here." her voice rung of confusion.

I ushered her inside the house, shutting the door to block off the cold breeze coming through. "Call me Jamie – oh yes. She gave me a call explaining that your family took a quick flight to Texas because your aunty is very sick and they didn't want to interrupt your night. So she asked if you could stay with us for awhile." her face showed no emotion, she just stood there like stone.

Macy's eyes flickered to the stairs before hiding her surprise, "Thank you for having me," she mumbled, she shuffled her feet nervously. The poor girl was a nervous wreck!

I smiled, "It's my pleasure, now where is that boy?" I mumbled before shouting for Blaze, "BLAZE!"

His cranky face popped out of his room, "What?" his dark hair sticking all over the place, his scowl which he inherited from his dad.

"We have a special visitor, come greet them!"

After a few shuffles and bangs Blaze emerged in boxers, his eyes widened as he saw Macy standing next to me, "What's she doing here?"

"She's staying with us for awhile – she'll be your new roommate," I pressed my lips to control my laugh from escaping. Blaze's expression was unreadable, "She what?" his eyes nearly buldged out like the size of golf balls.

Zane hugged me from behind, kissing me on the ceek. "You heard your mother – she's you roommate!"

"You don't have too-," Macy shyly muttered, her cheeks turning as red as her hair. Zane always disaproved of my matching but he had to admit the feelings for those two were so obvious!

I dismissed the idea, "Nonsense – Blaze is fine with it."

Blaze open and closed his mouth like a gold fish, eyes flashing between me and Zane. "Close your mouth boy!"

I waved them off, Blaze shot me an ungrateful look which I just ignored. "Goodnight!" I shouted as they trudged up the stairs. "I don't care what you do – just remember there's other people in the house," Zane chuckled as I began to laugh with him before lightly smacking him on the stomach.

"Shut up Dad!" Blaze yelled before slamming his door closed.

Macy P.O.V.

I glanced at Blaze who crankily walked past me before lying on his bed. I had remembered the look of his room from before, this time it was actually tidy. I placed my bag down against the wooden floor, i slowly walked over to his window where you could see my bedroom, "Blaze..." I started off but was cut off by him.

"Goodnight," he stated before switching off the lights. The only light was from the window, i stood there - my eyes rapidly blinking to adjust to the darkness.

"Uh... Blaze?" I whispered. I stood there awkwardly as the silence grew thicker, i let out a forced cough hoping Blaze would hear.

"What?" Blaze groaned.

"Where do I sleep?"

I could hear Blaze moving in his bed, "... on the floor."

I scrunched up my face, shooting him the finger which i knew he couldn't see in the dark. I let out a sigh before fumbling around for the light switch, I finally flipped it on, "I am not! Sleeping on the floor," I stomped up to his side poking him in the shoulder.

He buried his head into his pillow, "Sleep outside then." I continued to poke him, aiming for his stomach which made him squirm. Instead of getting up he rolled over, pulling the covers over him.

"Blaze!" I whined as I continued to shake him, i was not sleeping on the floor.

"Go away!"

"Let me sleep on the bed," I begged, i poked his ribcage the only response i got was a highpitch grunt.

He moved one centimetre, "There you go." He was still sprawled on the bed, i glanced at the spot - i could barely fit an arm there!

"I'm not sleeping in the same bed as you!" I protested.

"Well then don't complain about the floor."

"Blaze!" I continued to whine.

Blaze grabbed his pillow and tossed it at me, "Shut up!"

"Blaze!"

"Uh – fine," he grumbled as grabbed his pillow and a blanket tossing it onto the floor, he staggered sleepily out of the bed. Plonking on the hardwood floor, "Happy now?"

I smirke, "Yes, wasnt that hard now was it," i joked as i curled up into his bed. i snuggled in deeper - the soft material against my skin. I burried my face in my pillow, Blaze's familar smell overwhelming me.

I curled up drifting off to a peaceful sleep, where nothing bad could happen.

~

"Blaze! Turn off your damn alarm," I groaned as the persisting ringing continued.

I heard a few slams before the alarm went dead, out of the corner of my eyes I saw Blaze lying half dead on the floor. I snickered at how ridiculous he looked- his black hair sticking up in all places.

I began to drift off to sleep again, the sunlight was seeping through his curtains, "RISE AND SHINE BLAZEBOY!" a voice chirped, slamming Blaze's door opened.

"I thought I told you to turn the alarm off," I mumbled to Blaze.

"I did."

"Than-"

"Blaze? What are you doing on the floor – and why is there a girl in your bed?" the voice asked again.

I groaned to face the noisy girl, my eyes widened as she came into view. "Lucy – what are you doing here?" Blaze asked groggily as he got up.

"Why is this… ho here?" her eyes glared at me.

"Excuse me?" I propped myself on my elbow.

"You heard me bitch!"

I laughed, "If I'm a bitch how come you bark?" I retorted causing Blaze to snort.

"That's a failed comeback," she snorted twisting her golden hair in her fingers.

I moved so I was sitting up, my eyes glaring daggers into her, "Your mum's abortion was a fail," I snorted as I detangled myself from the bed sheets, "I'm going for a shower – control you dog," I stated before slamming Blaze's bathroom door shut.

The cold water splashed against my face, calming me down. I was tempted to march in there and slap that little bitch but I controlled myself. I inhaled as the water trickled down my back, I felt refreshed. I stepped out of the shower getting dressed and ready.

I was about to enter Blaze's room but I could hear them in deep conversation – I didn't mean to eavesdrop, but I couldn't help myself.

"She's got spunk – you guys are perfect!" Lucy snorted.

"She made me sleep on the floor," Blaze complained.

"That's why I like her!"

"Whose side you on?" Blaze teased.

Lucy's soft laugh echoed the room, "Your starting to fall for her... aren't you?"

Blaze ignored her "Do you think she was even jealous?"

"Yea I think she was, you guys are like Romeo and Juliet," she ended the sentence with a little aw.

"Shut up, and thanks again for playing along," Blaze muttered.

"Anything for my Blazey to find true love..."

"LUCY!" Blaze groaned before a few chuckles escaped.

I shut the door quietly, leaning against it. Their voices were swirling around in my mind, Jealous? Playing Along?

Then it all made sense, the scene last night and now. This was all Blazes' plan to make me jealous – he thought I was that easy to get. Oh now I wanted to slap Blaze. How could he? Did he think I had feelings for him? Okay so maybe I might have... at one point.

But I always reassured myself that it was lust, but as time kept on going I learned to like him more. But could it ever be love? I questioned myself. I shook my head, what a silly taught. I laughed at the idea of Blaze trying to trick me, I smiled to myself – it takes two to tango.

"Blaze hurry up!" Lucy shouted as me and she wondered through the market crowd. My plan had begun; I had 'apologized' to Lucy and offered for an outing to the local market. Lucy had her hand around my wrist as we continued to explore the market.

"This is really pretty," she held up a silver chain.

I admired it too, "You should buy it."

"OMG – it's like so pretty, do you think it match my hair," Blaze mimicked in a high pitch voice sending me into a fit of giggles while Lucy just smacked him, "Uncalled for."

"Wow, I love this," I muttered as my finger traced over a silver locket, I held it up as it began to shine against the light, "Beautiful," I could feel Blaze's breath tickling my neck, I put it back on the table, "Let's move on!"

Blaze gave me a puzzling look, "Aren't you going to buy it?"

"Nah – too expensive," I shrugged even though I'd sell my converses for it!

Lucy and Blaze began to lag behind a little, in a hush hush discussion making me feel quite anxious. Every so often they'd glance up at me. That's when I knew I had to my plan into action, for once I was doing a plan t hat Chloe hadn't come up with.

I walked a little faster, accident colliding into someone's hard chest. I looked up through my eyelashes to see a handsome guy peering down at me, next thing my hand was in his and he was pulling me up, "I'm sorry – it's just this pushy crowd," he gave me an innocent look as he ruffled his dark brown hair.

I felt a girlish giggle escape my mouth, "I understand." I whirled around to hear my name being called, Blaze's head bobbing through the crowd. I looked back at the mysterious guy then back at Blaze as he approached. I pulled the guys mouth against mine as I began to kiss him.

His lips moved in synch with mine not hesitating a moment. I was pretty caught up in the moment that was until someone ripped us apart, "What the hell Macy!" Blaze shouted at the confused guy and me. I entwined my fingers with guy whispering to him, "Go along with it."

"Nice to see you too Blaze," I smiled sweetly.

"What were you doing – swapping spit with this... imbecile," he gestured to the guy. I gave him a little squeeze and he soon returned, "He's not an imbecile!" I retorted.

"Who is he then?"

"My... my ur..." I hadn't thought this through.

"Her first love!" my mysterious guy saved me once again.

"I thought Aaron was your first love," Blaze mused.

"Well he is!" I stated.

"What his name?" Blaze was glaring at him.

"Its... ur..." I stuttered – this Is why Chloe does the planning.

"Liam, my names Liam. And who are you?"

"I'm Blaze – Macy's current boyfriend."

Liam then turned to Lucy who had been watching with curiosity and surprise the whole time, "And who is she?"

"My best-... I mean my ex-girlfriend," Blaze stumbled.

"Well then, let's go grab a coffee and you can tell me about how you guys met," Liam flashed everyone a smile as he draped his arm around my shoulder leaving a scowling Blaze stomping behind us.

A/N; Man its been ages since i uploaded. DONT KILL ME ;D hahah. Ive been busy with school and stuff. And i had writers block :'(Anyway i hoped you liked it - the next chapter will probably be upload soon.

I want to thankyou guys for the amazing support - i wouldn't be here without you. Oh and what do you think of LIAM ;DDD he's a babe

Peace out.

xWinglessx

Begging You To Stay - Chapter 16

Blaze p.o.v

I didn't like the way his arm snaked around her waist, occasionally pushing her hair away to whisper into her ear. Who was he? I had never even seen him in my life! The way she would flash him a smile, giggling at whatever he slurred to her.

"Blaze?" Lucy tugged on my sleeve, "What!" I snapped, my hands curling into fists.

She took a step back, "Well someone's been bitten by the jealousy bug!" her hands on her hips giving me a smug look. I rolled my eyes, i was so not in the mood to argue about this.

I watched as Macy and Liam waved us over from the seat they had snagged at the coffee house. They were sitting way too close for my liking, i grab Lucy's hand - clutching it. I let out a rough, forced laugh "im not jealous – I just have a ... suspicion about him, that's all."

"Liar."

Lucy slid into the booth, opposite Liam and Macy. I took another accusing look at them before slowly sitting next to Lucy. Lucy grabbed the menu from the side, shoving it in my face. I pushed it away, my eyes boring at Liam.

"So Liam, I've never seen you around school before, in fact even the town?" Like I was going to be nice to this... pretty boy! Ugh, i hadnt even seen him, yet mention him at all!

Liam ruffled with his hair, "Just came back from a trip to France where I was practising my French," he smiled politely before giving Macy a secret look.

"Why'd you guys break up?" I leaned forward eager to know, Macy eyes widened and she started squirm, she did this when she was anxious. "Well uh it just wasn't working," Macy coughed out, Liam on the other hand had another idea, "We were too in love, but I had to go on my scholarship while Macy had to stay back with her family and friends. Tragic love story don't you think?"

I was getting nowhere and no one was cracking and what is it with this Liam guy – is he always so... dramatic? It was Lucy who broke my train of thoughts, "I'll get the orders!" she took everyone's orders before scurrying off.

I was about to interrogate Liam some more when he suddenly got up and excused himself, "Forget to tell Lucy I want my coffee without sugar!"

When he was gone I gave Macy a stern look, "What the hell is going on! What are you playing at?" She just tilted her head and rested it on her palms, "Whatever are you talking about?" I nearly choked, "You and tightywhity guy were swapping spit!"

Macy chuckled, "Tightywighty? Wow, why are you jealous," she puckered her lips and pretended to kiss the air, I didn't know what to say – was i jealous? Macy rolled her eyes expecting me to say no. I surprised her, I surprised myself, "Yes."

Macy P.O.V

He said yes, Blaze never admitted to having any sort of feelings – why now? Just because I had a fake first lover who I'm pretty sure might just be gay? I shook my head, "What?" I asked Blaze, he just shook his head and whispered, "I guess I am... jealous."

"Did you ever think I was jealous of Lucy?" I muttered quietly. I knew where this was going and deep inside I was afraid. I looked anywhere but him, I was crap at confrontation – I could feel the blush rising in my cheeks, "I'm sorry," Blaze mumbled as his he caressed my cheek, I felt comfortable and I smiled.

"So what are we?" I asked Blaze, I was eager to know – were our feelings just lust or something more. "I don't know, but until we find out..." he leaned in, his brown eyes staring at me, that's when his lips met mine.

This kiss – it was different, at first I didn't kiss back but then it felt natural, right so I moved along with him. I never thought this would happen – me and Blaze, he was always so cold, so grumpy – but in the end he treats me right.

I moved my hand into his hair as he nibbled on my lip causing me to groan. "GET A ROOM!" someone shouted, I giggled pulling back, my face was all flustered and Blaze's cheeks were a tint of red. "Well I know a place!" Blaze winked at me, there was his old self, I rolled my eyes.

"Where's Liam and Lucy?" i glanced around the coffee shop but they were nowhere to be seen, "Maybe there hooking up," Blaze nudge my shoulder, I swatted him, "Should we go?" I turned to Blaze, he just nodded.

I followed Blaze as he led me down to the beach, we were both walking side by side, the sand sinking between my toes. I watched Blaze as he calmly watched the sea – as if it was something entrancing. I slowly slid my hand into he's to see what would happen.

At first he froze, I was scared – I had stuffed it up. But then he gripped onto my hand as if it was his safety rope and we kept one walking. I don't know how long we walked for but it was in silence – and it was the comfortable silence. No one had to say anything.

"Blaze?" I mumbled into his chest as his arms encircled my waist, "Hm?" He softly traced circles across my back, "Could we go home now?"

"Of course."

Maybe I was seeing a new Blaze, because here I was sleeping on his bed and without any protest he was sleeping on the cold floor. What was today? Thoughts kept running through my mind – was this all a dream?

I didn't want to know, I jolted up when I heard a pang. I waited, frozen – were we being robbed? After 5 seconds another pang, I slowly got up from bed, tip toeing around Blaze careful not to wake him. I edge towards the window and peeped out.

There he was, throwing rocks at my window. I shoved the window open as quietly asi could, "Aaron!" I whispered/shouted at the dark figure who was about to throw another rock. He froze, faced the sound of the noise.

"Oh shit, did I get the wrong house?" he said puzzled. I shook my head, "No, I'm staying at...." I paused – glancing over at Blaze, "I'm at a friends for the night," what would he think of Blaze?

"Can you come down? Please?" he begged.

I looked around the room, my eyes flickered over a peaceful Blaze. I muttered an apology as I grabbed my jacket and made my way to Aaron.

A/n; short i know ;O i did this in a rush when i was in the midst of packing. ^ ^ multi talentedness.

HAha; so im sorry im going on holiday- no internet access, unless i try and steal a computer ;O hahaha i doubt it!

But thankyou guys for your support. I know im crap at uploading - and i really am. :(

Chill out

xoxo

I'm Done Pretending - Chapter 17

Dedicated to my beautiful niece, your my inspiration for this chapter-

-A/N; some of this is written in third person - and i hope you like it-

Blaze P.O.V

I rolled over banging straight into the wall, I swore silently - being careful not to wake Macy. I clutched my head as I slowly got up - my head spinning with a hangover. I glanced at the bed, I expected her to be tangled in the sheets- hair sprawled everywhere.

But it was empty - unslept in, I had fallen asleep after her, so where could she be. I was fully awake now - searching the room for her, she had to be here. My eyes frantically searching in the dark, I paused over the window that was slightly ajar.

I could hear vague voices murmuring as the wind carried away their hush conversation, I could make out their figures a tall guy and a girl - I really wish it wasn't her, I really did. But as soon as light reflected from the streets, her red hair glowed before being swept by darkness.

I slammed the window shut; she was always going to go back to him - no matter how I tried to teach her, he just wasn't good enough for her. And along the process of this stupid revenge game, id fallen for her - more than I can possibly imagine.

~

Macy p.o.v

My head turned to the noise of Blaze's window shutting - I swear I saw a retreating figure, it was probably the wind, and I wrapped myself up in my jumper - the goose bumps on my arm running wild.

"What do you want Aaron?"

Aaron's eyes were tired, his eye bags were heavy - he gave me a tired smile, "I hope I'm not too late..."

"For what?"

"He's stolen your heart - it now belongs to him," his words were quiet but they echoed inside my head. I was going to interrupt him, make him take that back but I couldn't - because it was somewhat true.

"I know I lost my chance, you think the worse of me - but I need you to listen carefully to me," his eyes showed fear, regret, lost and mostly love - and it scared me, the hell out of me. He took my silence as a gesture to continue.

"You see - all the football boys were doing this stupid bet to see who could string along a girl the longest - at first I was all up for it, just for some fun. They picked you, I never really understood why but by the 3 week

I couldn't care because I'd met you," he paused, hatred and betrayal were screaming through my mind.

He continued, "I began to fall deeper and deeper into the lies, the bet was forgotten - all I needed was you, I had fallen for you Macy, and hard. But the guys knew I had won, so they said they'd give up the gig as soon as they outed you and me, expose the bet."

I was really tempted to slap him, it was game all along - the web of lies he spun continuously, he should have just told me the truth. I was screaming inside, but I patiently let him finish.

"So I dumped you, in the worse way imaginable so you'd hate me, forget about me so you wouldn't get hurt by the boys - because I care for you, I love you," his words got quiet, his eyes searching mine for forgiveness.

I took a step towards him, "I love you? Well did you ever think dumping me like that could hurt me? Oh because you were stupid enough to go along with those boys - what am I supposed to believe Aaron? What if this is another lie or bet? You should've just told me from the start, it's too late - I want nothing to do with you, anymore."

I snapped, it felt good - my head was spinning and my heart was pumping to the extreme - I finally said what I needed to say, Blaze would be proud. Blaze, what would he think of all of this - I was suddenly so desperate to retreat to his room.

Aaron was shocked but he knew, he knew he deserved this - he pulled me into a strong hug, I didn't hug back - I knew it still sent tingles up my spine and I hate that. I stood still as he hugged me, he whispered into my ear, his stubble brushing my cheek.

"I'm not giving up, he may have your heart - but I'm not giving up the girl of my dreams , not just yet," he vowed those words, his eyes glimmering with hope. He gave me a quick peek on the forehead before retreating.

I sighed as I watched him hope into his car and his headlights outlined the house and my shadow, I knew things were about to get way more complicated.

"Macy honey, wake up! You're late!" Mrs Morrisons honey coated voice rang through my head like an alarm bell; I rubbed my eyes before turning over to cover my face with the pillow, "Just five more minutes!" I mumbled.

"Its 8:50 darling." 8:50 - schools starts in 9, that's ten minutes. I snuggle my face deeper into the pillow before I bolt up realizing I am so. Freaking. Late. I jump out of the bed, mutter apologise and thanks to Mrs M before diving into my closet and pulling out anything to wear.

I can't believe Blaze didn't wake me up, speaking of the devil - where is he, I blush started to form on my cheeks as I remembered yesterday's events, "Where's Blaze?" I questioned as I skipped down the stairs while trying to put my boots on.

"He left already - quite early!"

"Shit..." I muttered to myself as I grabbed my skateboard and my bag, "See you late Mrs M!" I hollered as I shut the front door and half skated and half ran to school.

-

I slumped in my homeroom seat as soon as the bell rang, I had just made it here on time. "Mace you look like crap," Ryan sung as he took as seat next to me, I flipped him the finger, "I was late."

He chuckled, "Looks like someone needs to call the fashion police!" he poked his tongue out at me, he could be so immature, "Have you seen Blaze?" I totally ignored his rude remark, Ryan scrunched up his face - as if he was thinking hard.

"Uh - think he was on the field, he was just walking..."

"Thank you!" I grabbed my bag and bolted for the door, before pausing, "Ryan - tell Sir I'm here!" Ryan rolled his eyes, "Young love," he tutted.

-

Third Person p.o.v

Macy ran to the oak tree that overlooked the field, hoping she could catch a glimpse of Blaze. And sure enough she found him just walking around the field - kicking the random stones that lay on the ground.

"Blaze!" she shouted, her hands cupped around her mouth.

He just kept walking as if he hadn't heard her - but he did, and he just wanted time alone - to think, but she didn't know that. Macy quickly ran to catch up to him, her little legs pumping hard.

She was nearly out of breath as she approached him, her hand clasped on his shoulder - she was slightly bending over trying to get her breath back, "Blaze..." she huffed.

He acknowledged her with a solemn nod before continuing to walk away, she stood there in shock - what was he doing? Why was he so cold? She couldn't find the answer so she quickly kept up with his steps.

"Blaze, for god's sake - listen to me!" she stomped her foot as she planted herself right in front of him, "I don't know what crawled up your arse and died - but I demand for you to stop ignoring me!"

Blaze didn't crack a smile like he normally would, his face was expressionless - he was holding back the anger and emotion locked up, "Well, I'm not - so don't throw a tantrum," he said sarcastically, but it was harsh and it stung Macy.

"Why are you acting like this, after yesterday..."Macy's face desperately searched Blaze's as if to cling onto any remote memory of yesterday. Blaze looked at her in disgust, "Yesterday - want to talk about yesterday, how about whenever Aaron needs you - you go crawling back to him!"

Macy's whole world stopped, she had just dug herself her own grave - she wanted so badly to crawl in there and die, "Blaze, I didn't -," she stammered. He raised his hand to stop her, "Forget it, it meant nothing anyway."

Macy was shivering, she could feel her tears threatening to run wild - she was losing everything - life just wasn't fair. "But..." Blaze just walked past her, "I've got an exam to attend," he muttered before walking away.

He left Macy, who crouched down silently crying - she felt a conflict of emotions. She was seventeen she shouldn't have to deal with love, or heartbreak. Aaron had hurt her and claimed it was for good and she had learned to trust Blaze who just left her without any emotion in tact - her accusation and thoughts were going wild.

Little did she know that it was agony for Blaze to not go back to her and comfort Macy, it almost tore him apart.

A/N;

before you go killing Blaze or Aaron - give Aaron a chance, he ment well he's just retarded with emotions ?

And Blaze - you see his feelings in this one. Hope you can see and like this

xoxo

It's Too Late - Chapter 18

Merry Christmas !

"It's not you – it's me, biggest bullshit breakup line right there!" I mumbled through a mouthful of chocolate chip ice cream as I watched the continuous marathon of romantic dramas. I snuggled deeper into my warm bed, stuffing more spoonful's of ice-cream into my mouth.

"Where's Macy and what have you done to her?" a sweet voice echoed the room, I glanced up to see Selena, hand's on her hips – frowning at me. "Huh?" I questioned my mouth still full of ice cream. I heard a low snicker, "Looks like she ate her..."

A new figure had appeared in my room, with his feminie stance and accusative eyes I flipped him off, "I'm just watching tv..." lies, my rational voice hissed. Ryan snorted and snatched my ice cream away from me, "Hey!" I leaped at him, he just gracefully moved away – causing me to face plant.

Selena laughed as she curled up in my bed, "Stop mopping Macy, that's not going to get him back." I managed to get back onto the bed again, leaving my ice cream to a hungry Ryan, "Who? Aaron? Or Blaze?"

It was Ryan's turn to speak, "Ah little grasshopper – only time will tell, but until then your love won't wait forever," he murmured in a raspy wise voice, I threw my pillow at him, "Stop with your wise old man shit!"

"He's right though, you can't string them both along," Selena nodded, her blonde hair bobbing along with her head. "String?" my voice was now an octave higher. The bed dipped as Ryan made room for himself in the bed, "After what happened with Aaron, you're afraid to trust Blaze – like he might hurt you."

I ran my fingers through my knotted, wild red hair. I let out a frustrated sigh before burying my head into a pillow, "I can't let him go, both of them. I – i..." I groaned into my pillow, my voice muffled from the frustration.

Selena was soothing me by rubbing my shoulders just as my door slammed open and there stood the one and only Chloe – her hair messily pulled back into a ponytail, "Okay crew we've got a lot of work – Macy, I'm giving you ten seconds to get your fat ass out of bed!"

I pretended to not hear her demand as I tried to sink lower into my bed as possible. That didn't work as I curled up from the cold breeze that had hit me as Chloe yanked off my bed sheet. "Come on – I got tickets to the new twilight movie and you are not leaving me with those two emotion twihards," she point at Ryan and Selena.

I groaned, "I'm perfectly fine here..." I felt my body being physically dragged over to the mirror where they proceeded to discuss what a mess I looked like, I threw my hands up in frustration, "I'm right here!"

They only ignored me as they ushered me to get changed, they threw random items of clothing at me and shut the bathroom door right in my face. I let myself fall backwards onto the toilet lid, I buried my head in my hands, "Why cant life be easy..."

I didn't want to have to choose between Blaze and Aaron, Aaron thought me love and Blaze thought me trust, but which do I want. "I don't hear changing!" Chloe yelled through the bathroom door, I let out a breathy laugh – what would I do without my friends.

Blaze P. O.V

"Blaze!" Lucy yelled, I ignored her plea to stay, I was too god damn angry to give a shit. I was out the door within seconds, Lucy tugging on my leather jacket. I whirled around, towering over her, "What!" I snapped.

Lucy didn't seemed faze, she simply brushed a piece of hair out of her face, "Blaze, being angry isn't going to fix anything – go talk to her, she's a mess without you."

I threw my hands up in frustration, "Bullshit – she's probably running around with Aaron," I spat out his name like it was dirt – because he was. I pulled myself away from Lucy's grasp, her petite frame trying to hold me back.

"Please don't run from this – not again," her voice quiet and scared – I didn't want to leave but staying scared me, staying made feelings rise and for what? To just be hurt over again and again.

"I – I have to," I spoke softer this time, Lucy was like a sister – I never wanted to hurt her. She flashed me a sad smile, "You love her..."

"I don't."

"Then what is she to you?" Lucy asked.

"Nothing – just another easy girl," I sighed, it wasn't true – I just needed Lucy of my back. Lucy eyes wandered from behind me her smile suddenly wavering. I slowly followed her gaze, my eyes passing over dark eyes.

She froze, her red hair flying all over the place. She was wearing a light white sweater with brown shorts. She forced herself to smile as she walked over to the fence; Ryan, Selena and Chloe cautiously watching her carefully make her way to me.

Her eyes slowly tearing up as she flashed me a sad smile, I watched as she slowly kept her composure. " Just another easy girl, well Blaze it's great to know where we stand." Her eyes held no life as they left mine, guilt and fear started washing over me.

I watched as she walked briskly over to Chloe's car and slammed the door shut, her small bent figure in the back seat. What had I done? I let out a frustrated yell as the car pulled out of the driveway, I stormed away from Lucy and the house and yanked my car door open.

I started up the ignition without any thought, I just needed space. I slammed my foot onto the accelerator, not caring how fast I went because no matter what, my problems would still be here.

Chloe's P.O.V

I looked into the car mirror at Macy's hunched figure, it had taken me my whole might not to pound that insensitive asshole. Selena was trying her best to comfort her in the back but I knew Macy was beyond consolable.

I promised Lucy we'd try and get them back together but at this moment they both needed space, I turned into the cinema parking lot, killing the engine I turned to face Macy. "Hun, I know it hurts and you deserve so much better, don't let Blaze get you down – it's his lost."

She flashed me a gloomy smile, I felt my heartbreak seeing my best friend this sad but I kept up a cheerful front, Macy would hate to have her mood affect mine. I pulled Macy into a hug as Ryan and Selena ran to get our popcorn and drinks.

Macy slowly detached herself, "I- I've got to go clean up, be back soon." I gave her a quick smile and ushered her towards the female toilets. I groaned at the site of the multiple twilight pictures, it was like being in Selena's room.

"Well fancy seeing you here..." a low voice whispered into my ear, I nearly had attack and turned around to see the owner to the voice. There in his glory was Luke, I groaned – he was just everywhere nowadays.

"Go away Luke," I mumbled, turning back around and planning to ignore him. A few seconds had passed and he was still standing closely to me, "What do you want?" I hissed, last thing Macy needed was this ignorant idiot hanging around.

"Well you see, I have my eyes on this beautiful girl but she doesn't seem to be interested," he mused, I glared at him, "Unlucky for you," I stated dryly, I couldn't give a cow's arse about his love life. "She's an amazing kisser."

I pushed him away, "I don't care."

He leaned forward again, brushing a strand of hair from my face, "She also said I was a good kisser..."

"Luke," I warned him.

"Chloe," he murmured into the side of my neck, I froze – I couldn't think my head was going dizzy with all the crazy thoughts feeling my mind, all about Luke. I quickly pushed him away making sure no one saw, "Luke what happened at the party stays at the party."

"It was good to see you Chlo – hope we can chat again soon," Luke planted a kiss on my temple which I quickly wiped away as he slipped me a piece of paper with his number on it. I watched as he sauntered away to his group of girls.

I rolled my eyes, my hands paused over the trash can as the piece of paper was held loosely between my fingers. I retracted back and quickly stuffed his number into my pocket, I don't know what possessed me to do it, but it definitely did bring a cheerful smile to my face for the rest of the day.

Macy P.O.V

"Team Edward!" Selena screamed at Ryan who inhaled loudly before shouting "Team Jacob!" back at her. I groaned in my seat, this is what I get from being dragged to a twilight movie – normally Chloe would be complaining about how they never shut up but she seemed to be smiling.

A big smile, she thinks I don't know why – I chuckled to myself, I saw flirting with Luke. And that's good, Chloe always trying to match make people, well maybe she's found her knight in shining armour.

Her knight… my thoughts drifted back to Blaze, the way his eyes were hollow and sharp when he glared at me, no remorse or forgiveness left. No chance left, that had crushed me. I knew I should have done things differently but it didn't matter because I was just some other girl.

Some easy bang.

Aaron, he was amazing when he was him true self, but I hardly ever that true self unless it is just me and him. How am I supposed to know which Aaron I'm with, the jock Aaron or the sensitive one who reads Nicholas Sparks.

I let my eyes flutter close, finally I could escape – just for a moment, the hectic timeline I call my life.

~~~~~~~~~~

I rubbed my eyes open, I swear I had fallen asleep in Chloe's car but I glanced around the surroundings – this was my house. I had left Blaze's house with my stuff, mumbled quick apologizes to Mr and Mrs Morrison before fleeing back home.

My parents weren't due till this afternoon, I blinked a few times before searching for the time in my room. I opened my drawer, my face still buried in my pillow as I grasped around for my phone. My hand clasped around a rectangular shaped thing – I brought it up to see it was four in the afternoon

"Shit!" I mumbled to myself, quickly throwing myself out of bed and running down the stairs. I needed to pick my family up. I quickly dialled the cab number and ran outside, I paced back and forth waiting for the cab line to pick up.

"Macy?" my mothers voice rang, I glanced at the phone – it hadn't come from there. "Macy!" it shouted a little louder, I turned around to see my mother briskly walking towards me as she pulled me in for a close hug.

I breathed in her familiar scent of pinewood detergent and laughed as she mumbled how skinny I had gotten. She also immediately noticed the rings around my eyes, she let out a sigh, "Oh darling, whatever your decision – you have my support."

How'd she even know? I was asking the question to myself when mom spoke out loud, "Mothers know everything..." I gulped, "Even that time when..."

"Yes I know you broke my Japanese vase Macy, who else would try and glue it back together," Mom chuckled as she pulled me into another hug, "Wheres Felicity and Dad?"

"Right here!" Dad's voice boomed from the Morrisons yard, I gave mom a puzzling look which she quickly avoided. "Red head!" my little screamed as she ran into my arms, I picked her up spinning around in circles, "What do you eat, your so heavy!" I teased as she pouted.

Dad pulled me into a hug, "Good to see you kiddo – I'm sorry about Blaze."

"About what?" how did dad know, does dad know everything now? Dad quickly pretended not to here me and ushered Felicity into our house, my mother was shooting dangers at him. "What's going on?"

"Were sorry honey about Blaze, we know he'll fully recovers."

"Recovers from what?" what would Blaze need to recover from other than an over load of ego. Mum pursed her lips, her brow furrowed, "Oh honey! I'm so sorry, you didn't know – oh my, honey."

"Mom! Tell me! You're freaking me out."

"This afternoon – Blaze was in an accident, he's in a coma now..." She quickly pulled me into a hug as the news slowly sunk in, my body began to shake as tears were spilling out – I couldn't lose him, especially not on the terms we were.

"He's in Wesley Hospital – go, go see him," She gave me a small smile before leaving me out alone by the fence, where about 7 hours ago Blaze stood before me, alive and well.

A/N; I have finally updated, Merry Christmas, my present to you. Stay safe and have a wonderful day with your friends and family. Take care

xo

Chasing Fate - Chasing 19

Okayy ; read on and i hope you like it :D

Macy's P.O.V

"Pick up, pick up," I muttered into my phone, why wasn't Chloe picking up! I paced back and forth. My car just had to be at the mechanics. I needed to get to the hospital and fast! I pressed the end button on the call, scrolling down my contacts list I paused.

Aaron...I let out a sigh, I imagined a lifeless Blaze, no mysterious blue eyes peering back at me, pale skin attached with multiple wires. My eyes shot open, my chest rising up and down – without hesitating and I pressed call.

I pressed my ear to the receiver; the line quickly picked up – static and background noise attacking my ear. A breathless voice answered, "Hello?"

"Aaron – can you give me a lift?" my voice was soft, I don't know if I could hold on any longer. What if Blaze died, I would never get to tell him how I feel – I'd lose him! Aaron perked up, he had picked up on my voice, "Macy! What's wrong? What happened?"

I persisted on, "I'll tell you later, just please come to my house. Hurry!" I could hear Aaron running down his stairs, his heavy breathing into the phone. I willed for Blaze to hold on. 'I'll be right there Mace, stay put." With that the phone clicked off.

I let my hand drop from my ear to my side, dangling lifelessly. I remember the first time I met Blaze, running into him in the library. The memory slowly brought tears to my eyes.

I laughed, shooing Chloe and Ryan away, "I'll meet you at the stands, just got to put these books away!" they nodded as I collected the books. I snuggled into Aaron's football jersey that only the footballer's girlfriend could wear. It made my heart lunge every time – that Aaron had picked me to wear his jersey.

I shoved the books into the vacant shelf, hurrying myself so I wouldn't miss the game. I was about to leave when I heard a soft voice travel from the courtyard – being the curious person I was, I peeked around the corner.

His black hair fell over his face, his fingers carefully strumming an acoustic guitar, his eyes shut tight while he hummed a familiar tune. My hand came to rest on the railings; something about him had a pulling force. Without looking up he spoke, "Aren't you supposed to be at the game?"

I jumped back from his sudden question, "I-I'm on my way there…"

The silence faded as the dark haired boy begin to strum louder, "if I lay here, if I just lay here – would you lie with me and just forget the world?" his voice was raspy yet soothing, I felt somewhat entranced – like he was speaking directly to me.

"A-are you new to the school?" I stuttered, I'd never seen him before. He didn't stop strumming, he simply opened his eyes, "I don't quite know, how to say. How to feel…" he continued singing, I let out a quiet gasp at the sight of his blue eyes.

"Your late, I don't think your boyfriend will be too happy," he spoke, his voice knocking me out of a trance. I quickly gathered up my stuff giving him a quick nod, I caught a quick glance of him as I left he had returned back to singing.

I rushed out of the library, my heart was beating like crazy, first of all I was late for Aaron's game and secondly that was the first day I met Blaze Morrison.

"Macy!" he enveloped me in his arms, I buried my face into his chest – the familiar smell of his cologne helping me to breath. I let the tears slowly flow, he didn't even mind I was getting his t-shirt wet. "I've lost him – I can't!" I wailed, Aaron muttered soothing words to me, rubbing circles on my back.

"Come on Macy – how about you explain to me in the car?" I lifted my head up, staring into Aaron's eyes – I managed a small smile. That used to be Aaron that held me world in his hands – but now the guy who held my world was trying to cling onto his own.

Chloe p .o. v

"Fancy seeing you here Chlo!" I silently cursed my aunt, she needed a hand at her local café so I agreed- thinking it would be a good way to earn some extra money. I never imagined I would be harassed.

"Luke – go away."

"Is that anyway to serve a customer?" his smirk was barely containable, he was always mocking me with those eyes, evil eyes. I grabbed a menu before shoving it hard into his hands, "Considered yourself served, goodbye Luke," I said deadpanned, hoping he caught the drift that I didn't want to stay and chat.

I forced a smile as I refilled a lady's cup with coffee. I placed it back on the table for a refill as I wiped my hands on my apron. A warm breath tickled my ears, causing me to shiver, "Did it hurt?" he murmured, his lips slightly pressed against my neck.

I let out a gasp, "huh?"

Luke pulled away, "When you fell from heaven," he chuckled, I whirled around slapping him straight on the chest, "Don't you dare use your cheesy pickup lines on me!"

"It worked the other night…" I clamped my hand over his mouth, "Would you shut it! This is my aunts café, do you want me to be locked up in a castle never to see daylight again?"

"Oh Rapunzel, Rapunzel let down your hair," Luke wiggled his eyebrows at me before grabbing the ready coffee pot and making his way to a couple awaiting a refill. I grabbed the wash basket, grabbing empty plates and cups. I rammed my hip into Luke, "Can't you just leave me alone?

He bit his lip, "Nope!"

I groaned in frustration, "What have I ever done to you!"

"One date, tomorrow at 4! Then ill promise to leave you alone."

I raised my brow at him, "That's even worse."

"You'll never have to see me again," he baited. I silently cursed him, "Fine – one acquainted meeting, not date. Meeting," I emphasised the last word giving him a stern look.

Luke eyes lit up as he shoved the coffee pot to a passing lady, he murmured something to himself before exiting the café, "I got a date with Chloe – suckers, I'm getting laid!" I heard him yell from outside, I shook my head in disbelief, too bad I couldn't shake the smile.

Aaron's P.O.V

She was curled up in the passenger seat, her head bent. It scared me to see someone so full of life slowly being drained. I wasn't too pleased with the idea of sending her back into prince charming's arms, but she needed me – and I was only too happy to oblige.

The old static radio hummed through the silence, I wanted to say something but I was afraid of hurting her – she looked so fragile. It hit my window screen, a tiny raindrop followed by another 10 then slowly hundreds. I pulled into the hospitals car park, grateful that it hadn't been raining too heavily.

"Macy..."

Her head flew up, her big brown eyes wide in alarm. I slipped my hand into hers and gave it a gentle squeeze, "Were here..."

Macy flashed me a sad smile, "Thank you Aaron, i know it was hard for you to bring me here but thanks." I watched as she let go of my hand, getting out of the car – rain immediately pouring down on her.

I watched her walk away, the colder I felt. I quickly got out of the car, slamming the door – running after her, my feet splashing in the puddles. "I get it, he's hurt but Macy he's just using you," I couldn't give up – I couldn't lose her. I made the mistake once and I wasn't plan on doing it again.

She stopped, I could feel the rain seeping through my shirt. She slowly turned around, her red hair already drenched, "You don't get to say that... YOU have no RIGHT! You were the one who broke my heart, you handed me right to Blaze," she snapped, I could see her shaking.

I clutched my fist, "Me? I taught you how to love! Without me you would be nothing!" I regretted the words as soon as they left my mouth. Her eyes snapped open, she began shaking with laughter, "Nothing? No that's right you taught me how to hate and to realise that you're just an idiot!"

"Oh did Blaze teach you how to suck his dick?" I was too darn angry to care anymore – I loved her but right now she was too blinded by that dumb idiot. She walked straight up to me, tears were falling from her eyes. Macy lifted up her hand as she striked my cheek, "I want the old Aaron back – the true one. When you find him – let me know, because that's the guy I love – as a friend now Aaron. As a friend."

I brought my hand up to my cheek, the rejection definitely stung more than the slap. I pulled back – I had pushed her, instead of into my arms i pushed her into Blaze's. I let out a sigh, "Does he make you happy?"

Macy paused, her eyes wavering, "Yes, he does… and one day there will be girl out there who makes you truly happy." She pulled me into a hug, I wrapped my arms carefully around her never wanting to let go. But I eventually had to; I stood there as the rain soaked me watching the girl who made me truly happy walk away.

I let the moment past, it was too late for me to be her prince charming.

Macy p.o.v

The fight with Aaron had drained me more, I was dripping with water, my skin had Goosebumps. I could feel my teeth chattering. I ignored the stares from the patients as I trudged to the information desk, leaving wet footprints on the ground.

The lady with the glasses perched on her nose looked up, "Oh dear! Hold on hun, I'll get you a towel." I watched as she quickly left only to re-enter with a white fluffy towel. I wrapped it around me, trying to dry off, "Thank you – um do you know which room Blaze Morrison is in?"

She nodded, "Are you a family member?"

I racked my brain – what was i? And didn't they only let family into ICU, "His sister…" the lie rolled off my tongue. The lady nodded, "Go up to level two and follow the signs to ICU, they'll take you through there."

I gave her a big smile, "Thanks again!" Wrapping the towel around me tighter I practically ran into the elevators, impatiently rocking on my heels. I watched as the buttons lighted up, the doors opened on level one to let an old man in a wheel chair in before it closed and open up to level two.

I hastily walked towards the arrow that pointed down the hallway to ICU. My breath began to catch on my throat as I walked to the ICU front desk, I could see the patients through the white doors. "I'm here to see Blaze Morrison – I'm his sister."

The nurse nodded before getting up and swiping her card, the doors immediately parted. She beckoned me to follow – she brought me to a big sink with multiple soap bottles, "Wash your hands please, we try to provide our patients with a germ free environment."

I pumped a whole clump of soap into the palm of my hand, washing furiously – I needed to see Blaze. When I was finished the nurse led me through the corridors before stomping outside a room, she pushed back the curtain to reveal a lifeless body connect with wires.

My breath was caught in my throat, I grabbed nurses arm trying to keep my balance as tears flowed. I watched as the machines helped him breath, no blue eyes accusing me. Just a pale Blaze… My eyes drifted towards the heart monitor. Its smooth beeping rhythm seemed to calm me down, he had to wake up!

He couldn't just leave me, I reached for his hand – cold and clammy just like I expected. I brought his lifeless hand up to my lip, before I could plant a soft kiss. The heart monitor stopped, only to sound with a surprising alarm.

I was jolted away from him as the nurses and doctors piled into the small single room; they kept pushing me further and further away from Blaze. I felt myself fall, I refused to lose him, the guy I loved.

Realising The Truth - Chapter 20

Yes ive uploaded, yes im a lazy butt and i havent done it in a while i am truly sorry.

enjoy

There's always a time where you'll wonder, what if? What if I hadn't said those things to do that person, would it be different? We can't help but blame ourselves for what mistakes we let happened. It just felt like the same mistakes, different situations.

I never liked to wait, I was impatient when I was a little kid – never could really wait my turns in the lines to the canteen. So waiting for Blaze to come out of surgery was even harder. I watched Mr Morrison pace back and forth while Mrs Morrison was quietly sitting down. You could see a lot of Blaze in the both of them, Blaze inherited Mrs M's eyes while he got his father's cheek bones.

Blaze thought no one cared about him, he doesn't know how much people do. I could feel the Styrofoam cup in my hands being crushed as seconds seemed like hours. "Macy! Omg we came as soon as we could, is he alright?"

Chloe came rushing in, still in her Aunt's café uniform, Lucy right behind her.

Lucy rushed over to Mr Morrison; her eyes were rimmed red as her face was extremely pale. "His heart stopped... he's in surgery... Chloe I know you don't like him but I just can't lose him! He may be a goofball, but he's my goofball." I was bawling my eyes out now, sobbing like a mad cow.

Chloe gave me a fragile smile before enveloping me into a hug, "Aw hun, I don't hate him – if anything he made you happy! And it has taken you this bloody long to realize you guys like each other!"

I pulled away, giving her a funny look through sobbing. She just wrapped me into another hug, "Does he make your heart race?"

I scrunched my forehead together, thinking back to all those times me and Blaze had. The stupid arguments and the endless bantering – to the kisses, I let out a sigh, "Yes."

"Do you trust him?"

I bit my lip, remembering all those plans that Chloe put us through, he had managed to stick by them, helping me no matter what. I gave Chloe a small nod, she continued on, "If he was with another girl..."

My grip around Chloe's hand tightened – I remember when Lucy and Blaze had put on that act to see what I would do, I remember all those girls he'd go on dates with – and I was just some act. It made my blood boil, I wanted to be one of this girls – I hoped I was.

My eyes tears as I remembered his word, "Just another easy girl," that's all I was to him. My mouth felt dry as the saltiness from my tears stung. "I wouldn't know what to do, and besides what's the point – I'm just some easy girl, remember?"

Chloe didn't speak she just stood, her hands gripping hard onto my shoulders. "You listen here Macy," a soft voice spoke, Lucy was now standing next to Chloe, her face almost drained of life.

"I've known Blaze since diaper days, he changed after his sister death – yes he pushed everyone away but you seem to manage to bring a spark of life back to him. Blaze is a quitter and has major trust issues and for him to even tell you about his sister let alone stick with you through this who revenge plan says A LOT. Now get some sense into you, the way the boy looks it you is bloody obvious – he's fucking in love with you!" Lucy was nearly out of breathe when she finished her speech, her eyes narrowed before softening, "Just don't let him go..."

"Lucy! Did you just swear?" I heard Mrs M ask in shock. Lucy flashed her an apologetic look. I pulled Lucy into an unexpected hug, her watermelon perfume overwhelming me, "Thank you, I just needed someone to make me see straight."

Lucy let out a muffled laugh, "It's alright, the boy would have probably told you himself if he had any balls," she grumbled before marching over to the vending machine. I gave Chloe a snort, that girl was quite a character but I really did admire her.

"Morrison family?" a tired voice spoke, he was wearing the surgeons uniform, glasses pushed down to the bridge of his nose. His eyes searching the room, I watched as the Mr and Mrs M made their way to him. I buried my face into Chloe's neck, I couldn't watch.

"Macy."

"Macy!"

I shut my eyes, life seems better not knowing any news. Not knowing if it was bad or good, because my reaction would depend on the news that the surgeon held – and I expected the bad. "Mace! He's in icu, stable condition," Chloe's voice rung into my ears, I let out a breath of relief as tears began to flow again – god I was an emotional wreck.

"It's alright, come on lets go get some coffee in you," Chloe soothed as she directed me from the icu unit.

Chloe's p.o.v

"Is she alright?" Ryan asked, his voice booming through loud speaker. Selena chimed in, "Yeah I feel so bad I haven't gone to see her, things have been major busy!"

I clamped then straightener bringing it down watching my blonde hair straightened, "She hasn't gone home in 2 days, I tried but she's so stubborn." I sighed, ever since the hospital let non family visit Blaze she had slept there.

"Oh, ill bring some lunch to her later," Ryan murmured, I could hear him rustling around in his kitchen – pots and pans banging. "Yes please check up on her, I cant today because I just got back from work and now I have to go to my funeral." I rolled my eyes, my date with Luke.

"Funeral?!" Selena squawked. I let out a snort, "Hypothetically, I've got a date with Luke."

"Elton John say what?" I heard the sound of a loud crash as Ryan yelled through the receiver. "I wouldn't call it date, more like a ..."

"Meeting?" Selena suggested, I grunted as I glanced in the mirror. I wore a plain summer tee with shorts. I wasn't going to look like a pig or get overdressed – it was just Luke. "But yeah back to Mace, im really worried – I heard the doctors talking about Blaze. They think he might have a chance of brain injury."

"I swear to god, if he wakes up like in The Vow and has no memory of Mace im going to punch him till her remembers," Ryan threatened sending Selena and me into fits of giggles, "Oh tough guy," Selena joked, laughter still ringing through the call.

I let out a sigh, "But yeah, just they both don't deserve this."

Ryan and Selena both agreed, Blaze was right for Macy. "OI CHLOBEAR!" a voice shouted before a hasty car honk sounded. I threw my window open, head peering outside. I grimaced as I saw the black jeep parked by the side of the road, Luke's head sticking out of it.

"CHLOE'S NOT HOME!" I yelled back, grabbing my purse and shoes. "HURRY UP PRINCESS! WE HAVE RESERVATIONS!" I could Ryan and Selena gossiping, I ignored them, "Go see Mace, now bye."

"Good luck! Bye," the both muttered before I hung up. I ran down the stairs, saying goodbye to mum before I was out the door. "Reservations for what?" I slipped my heels on, adjusting my top. He got down, blue eyes wondering all over me – I watched as he opened the passenger seat like a gentlemen. "Reservations to my bed."

I gave him a sharp look, "Well looks like your gonna have reservations ALONE." He let out a silent laugh, pinching my cheek as I attempted to swat his hand, "Im sorry Chloe, but your so adorable to mess with."

I put my foot into the car, swinging myself onto the seat, "Just let's get this done and over with," I snapped before slamming the door shut in front of his face.

No one's p.o.v

Her red hair was sprawled messily as she lay back in the plastic chair, her eyes tempted to close. She was fighting her sleepiness, coffee in her hand – she couldn't miss the moment when Blaze woke up, that is if he woke up…

She ran her hand over her face, desperately trying to refresh herself. The small tv across the room blared some black and white film with Charlie Chaplin. Macy tucked her feet onto the uncomfortable chair; she'd been sleeping on this thing for the last 2 nights.

Her eyes flickered over to a pale Blaze, his dark hair made his face seem even more ghost like. No blue eyes were there to great her, no smug look there to say, "I got laid." Just no Blaze, she was tired from crying, only red rims signified any sign of crying.

Macy let out a sigh as she leaned over and clutched Blaze's hand, "I probably won't do this if you wake up because I'm a chicken but I want you to know that you changed my life. And thank you for becoming the worst and best thing in it, thank you for being someone I can trust. Thank you for being an amazing fake boyfriend."

Macy placed a kiss on his cold forehead; she squirmed as she dodged the wires connected to his body. She placed her clammy hand over his hand again, "Wake up tomorrow!" she whispered as she snuggled into the side of the bed, her eyes closing.

Look After You - Chapter 21

A/N: Well Ollie makes an appearance in trhis chapter, if you dont remember thats Blaze's dead little sister. No this is not one of thos fantasy ghost. And Just to let you know, the story wiill come to an end in about 4 or 3 more chapters with an epilogue.

There might be a sequel, but Blaze and Macy would only make occasional experiences.

But anyhoo, enjoy. My favourite chapter so far = id say.

Chapter 21

The blackness started to fade and was slowly being replaced by a strong bright light. I blinked rapidly to keep the bright light from stinging my eyes. I sat up as soon as my vision cleared, I was greeted by a bland white room. Where the hell was i? "Finally your awake!" her soft voice spoke, I whirled around – there she was, in her favourite white summer dress, still the same height and those same blue eyes.

"Ollie?" my dead baby sister couldn't be standing right in front of me, I reached – my hand landed upon on her shoulder – she was real. "Oh shit," I murmured before I pulled her into a big hug, the realisation of how much I miss her everyday hit me, I could feel tears starting to stream down my face.

"Stop crying you big softie!" she pulled away from the hug, she had her familiar smirk on her lips- gosh she was just how I remembered. I let out a sad smile, she would never grow older because she died – she would never grow up to have kids or a husband. The sudden thought bit at me coldly, making me squirm.

"Wait... Ollie your dead though. That means – omg is this heaven?" everything was white, I blame all those stereotypical movies for my current freak out. Ollie just raised a brow, "You think you'd go to heaven, nice joke Blaze. You're in a coma, you died twice – but you're hanging on."

My mouth opened before closing again, "Gah." That was the only sound that managed to come out. This was really too much to comprehend and let alone it coming from my 9yr old sister. She just stared, "I like Macy."

"You know about her?"

Ollie just shot me a deadpanned look, "I like her too." That's when a sharp pain stung my cheek, I glanced at Ollie who had just slapped me, "What the heck Ollie!" she may be nine but I'm pretty sure she hit pms already.

"You're the idiot who said those hurtful words to her! I mean are you serious Blaze, then you go ram your car into a tree – everyone's bawling their eyes out for you!" That's when my memory came flooding back, Macy's hurtful face the next minute there was blood everywhere before it all faded out.

"Oh."

"And how could you be selfish! Mum and Dad! There so scared, after losing me... they can't lose you Blaze," her voice toned down, her eyes started to water. I didn't even realised how much I would hurt mum and dad, I felt like the biggest arsehole right now. I pulled her into a big hug, bearing my face into a shoulder – I could feel her tears soaking through my shirt, "I'm so sorry Ol, I'm so sorry."

She sniffled, pulling away, "Don't apologise to me! You owe them to others."

I glanced at her, when had she matured so much, "Ollie, I'm sorry for when I didn't save you – how I watched as you got hit by that car. I've never forgiven myself, it was my fault and I'm so sorry – you'll always be my baby sister, I've never forgotten you."

Ollie just smiled, ruffling my hair – since I was squatting to be her height. "It wasn't your fault; i haven't forgiven you because there's no reason for you to be sorry in the first place! You were the best brother anyone could ask for and what's hurting me is that you're here when you have an amazing life to live."

Relief flooded through me, all these years – but I somewhat felt better to hear her say them. Since when did she get so wise, "What were you, Ghandi in your past life?"

She scrunched up her nose, "You're so weird, I don't even know who you're talking about." I rolled my eyes, and pulled her into one last hug, "Well thank you Ollie, you always knew the right things to say." I could already feel myself drifting from her and this place – like I wasn't supposed to be here.

"Can you do me a favour?" her blue eyes were full of hope, I nodded, "Of course." She leaned in and whispered into my ear before I felt myself completely fade and everything went black.

Macy's P>O>V

"He's awake!" the doctor announced, Mr and Mrs Morrison's faces flashed with relief as they hurried towards their sons room. Those two words sunk into my brain, I let my head fall back onto Lucy's shoulder, she was sobbing quietly, her shoulder vibrating.

"You should go see him first," I mumbled towards Lucy, she was his best friend – the last person he wanted to see was me. Lucy wiped her fallen tears, her red eyes looked into mine, "Let's go in together," her hand enveloped mine, her voice was fragile and rough. We both haven't slept in 3 days.

I squeezed her hand, "Come on then," I got up, pulling her up to. We slowly made our way the same way the Morrison's had, my feet seem to numb the closer we got – my heart beat was increasing rapidly. Lucy pushed the door open, Blaze was pale as ever but his blue eyes were attentive and wandering around the room, landing on me. I glanced quickly away – I let Lucy's hand go as she rushed to hug Blaze.

Mr and Mrs Morrisons faces were beaming, they were obviously dead tired but relieved to see their son alive. Mrs Morrison gave me a quick hug before they left the room. Lucy was gushing over Blaze, I stood awkwardly at the back of the room – I really wasn't ready for this.

Lucy looked up, she bit her lip, "I just remembered I had to call mum about something, well I'll be back soon," Lucy mumbled before she winked at me and dashed out of the room before I could stop her. She was as manipulative as Chloe.

It was just Blaze and me in the room now, I finally got the courage to look at him – I let out a small gasp, he was already staring at me – blank expression but his eyes said it all, and just like that he was forgiven. I approached him, I gently sat down on his bed – careful not to injure him.

"How you feeling?"

He continued just to stare at me before he spoke, "Do I know you? Have we met before?"

My eyes widened, "No no no!" I muttered, this couldn't be one of those shows where the love of the life forgets you – just like in The Vow. I started to panic, my breathing was harsh as I gripped Blaze's hand, "You have to remember me you idiot! I haven't even got to tell you I love you and there you go – getting amnesia. Do you know how worried I was? I haven't slept for 3 days, god and let me tell you those plastic hospital chairs hurt like a bitch and-"

I was silence when a pair of lips smashed into mine, his soft lips were against mine – I could feel my anger and frustration fading, he always had this effect on me. My heart started to beat faster, the way he made me feel when we kissed, all warm and fuzzy on the inside. He gently pulled away, my hands flew up to my lips, they were still tingling.

"I was joking, of course I remember the girl I love," his voice was hoarse, but he wore the same lopsided grin. The anger returned, I slapped him hard on the chest, who cares if he just got out of surgery – the idiot had me worried sick!

"How could you! You idiot! You stupid monkey donkey butt face!" I slapped him harder, I could hear Blaze chuckling, he grabbed my hands as I continued to struggle, he was still so strong. "Macy, repeat what I just said."

I gave him a confused look but did what he said, I swear he's gotten brain damage, "You said: 'I was joking, of course I remember the girl I love...'"

That's when it hit me, and Blaze let go of my hands, "You... you love me?" tears were forming, gosh this boy had me go through all 10 different emotions in the past 10 minutes. He let out a sigh, he leant back on his pillow, "You're annoying, tiring and downright clumsy but your also beautiful, charming, intelligent and I love you."

I let out a squeak of joy. That was probably the most romantic thing anyone has ever said to me. I buried my face into his nook of his shoulder, "I love you too, you ass." He chuckled as he pulled me closer to him, pressing his cold lips against my forehead.

No One's P.O.V/

Blaze was extremely tired but content – throughout the day, many people had visited and he'd been grateful but he was happy now because Macy was back by his side, snuggled into his side. The nurses changed his drips before leaving him and Macy alone.

"Mace?" he gently shook her, he wasn't sure if she was awake not. Macy's eyes were closed, but she was just resting, content in Blaze's arms. "Yeah?"

"Well this is going to sound weird..." he trailed, but he was going to do it – for Ollie. Macy propped her head up, she stayed silence – he continued, "Well you see, when I was out cold – I had this kind of dream thing. Except it wasn't a dream, like I saw... Ollie."

Macy let out a soft gasp, before she composed herself. This was important for Blaze and she was going to listen. "What... what did Ollie say?"

Blaze bit the inside of his lip, "She said, she gives us our full blessing to elope." Blaze blushed tomato red, it looked hilarious on the pale face Blaze – Macy was already chuckling, her stomach starting to cramp. She placed a soft kiss on Blaze's nose, she knew this was important to him. "Well I would be honoured to have Ollie as my sister-in-law."

Blaze let out a sigh of relief, and pulled Macy closer. Ollie was right, she was a keeper. Everything in his life had sorted out, from his past to maybe his future. But he had learnt that life is precious and so are the people in it.

My Prince Charming - Chapter 22

Warning: Includes extreme cliche and cheesyness in this chapter.

Only a few more chapter left; omfg. My baby's growing up D':

Blaze's P.O.V

"UP AND ATOM!"

I groaned and squished my eyelids tighter trying to ignore the bright sun seeping through the curtains. I daringly opened my eyes to see a happy Ryan standing in front of my hospital bed, god knows what he's wearing...

I suddenly remember Macy, I quickly glanced down at my arms to see her curled up in my arms – sleeping peacefully. I stifled a laugh at how ridiculous her red hair looked all over the place. She groaned, her eyelids fluttering, "Go away Ryan!" she muttered before snuggling closer to me.

I chuckled, "Dude, who wakes people up like that anyway?" I haven't heard anyone say "Up and Atom in ages..." Ryan raised an eyebrow, "How about shake a leg?"

I shook my head, that one didn't even make sense. Ryan glanced around before his face lit up with excitement, "Let's have you lazy daisy..."

Before Ryan could even finish Macy had thrown a pillow at him, "Worst one yet, Ryan why are you even here?" Macy was rubbing her face, note to self: she's not a morning person! Ryan gasped, "Can't a best friend want to see his favourite couple at 7am and not have a motive?"

Macy flipped him the finger, "7am! For god's sake Ryan!"

Ryan rolled his eyes, "I'm actually here to get rid of you, Blaze and I have to do some man to man chatting!" Macy scoffed, "Ryan, there is no need to man to man chat to Blaze!"

Ryan plonked himself down on the end of the bed, he smiled, "Yes there is! Now go, Chloe and Selena are waiting for you outside!" I glanced anxiously at Macy, don't get me wrong I'm not a homophobe and Ryan's a cool kid but sometimes he scared the crap out of me.

As soon as Macy got up from the bed, Ryan took her place before slinging his arm around my shoulder. My eyes connected with Macy, I mouthed to her as Ryan babbled on about America's next top model show. "Help me!"

Macy just shook her head laughing, before mouthing back, "Nope!" I watched as her red hair disappeared out the door and Ryan stopped talking. "Good, she's gone now... Now Blaze, I'm thinking romantic dinner for Mace?"

I bit my lip, I didn't quite follow. Ryan noticed my confused because he explained, "When Macy was with Aaron, he really didn't quite care about the whole romantic gestures so I thought since you guys both confessed your love for each other you know you could…"

My lips formed an O shape, "So you want me to do a romantic dinner for Mace, now?"

Ryan just smiled and nodded, pleased with himself.

"But were in a hospital?"

Ryan clasped his hands together, "Isn't it romantic, the injured lovers reunite-" Ryan kept on babbling I just nodded and smile, it was only 7:15… it was going to be a long day…

"Blaze are you even listening?"

Chloe's P.O.V.

"What's Ryan up to?" Macy raised her eyebrow at me. I laughed, "It's Ryan, the boy isn't afraid to dress up as a naked cupid, he could be up to anything!"

Selena chortled, "Yeah Blaze is a dead man!"

Macy just laughed, "Enough about Blaze and I, what's been going on with you guys?" Selena just shrugged, "Nothing interesting, not compared to Chloe," her eyebrow raised and she nudge me in the stomach. I watch as Macy's eyes widened and they both leaned forward, begging me to spill.

"I had a date…"

Macy slapped my arm, "With who?"

"Luke…"

That's when a sharp sting hit my arm, I groaned grabbing my arm, "Mace!" she rolled her eyes like she hadn't just slapped me hard, "Why didn't you tell me?! This is great Chloe," she shot me a bright smile.

"Well because you had so much going on and well it wasn't really a date I mean..."

"Was it the two of you?" Macy asked.

I nodded, Selena leaned closer, "Was he sweet?"

"Yes..."

Macy had her hands clasped together, "Did he pay for everything?"

"Maybe..."

Selena giggled, "Did you guys kiss?"

"..." I felt my cheeks grow warm, I avoided there stares as their eyes widened and their mouths dropped open. I nearly screamed as the both slapped my arm as they squealed with excitement, "CHLOOEE'S GOT A BOYFRIEND!" Macy hollered as she sat there grinning at me like a maniac.

"Luke and Chloe sitting in a tree-," Selena began as Macy chimed in, I let my head lean back as I groaned, I regret telling them. I jolted straight back up when I heard a deep yell and I saw a fear stricken Ryan ran out of Blaze's room.

"I WILL STUFF YOUR HEAD UP YOUR ARSE!" Blaze's voice raged as Ryan ran as fast as his skinny jeans let him; i glanced at the girls before we all keeled over laughing. That's what Ryan gets for trying to interfere.

Macy's P.O.V.

"Okay seriously, can I take the blindfold off yet?" after lunch Selena and Chloe had both kidnapped me and shoved me into a white dress I'd never seen before my life and then proceed to blindfold me. Chloe laughed as she continued to lead me, with my eyesight blinded all my other senses grew, "Do I smell chicken?"

"Do you ever stop thinking about food?"

That voice had butterflies erupting in my stomach, I knew why I was blindfolded and I knew Ryan was also behind this but I didn't care, because I got to spend it with him and that's the best present anyone could give. Chloe fiddled with the blind fold before it dropped and I blinked a couple of times before I adjusted to the scene before me.

We were in the hospital cafeteria, Blaze was in front of me in his wheel chair, the sight of him so different, it hurt to see him so fragile. I gasped, the lighting was dim but the strongest glow came from the table situated in the middle of the room, roses in the middle and a dinner set for two.

I could feel tears in my eyes, "Blaze..."

Blaze just shot me a cheesy grin, "Ryan's wanted you to have you a romantic dinner, and well I thought this might do?"

"It's beautiful," before I could bend down to hug Blaze, Ryan had intervened and placed an acoustic guitar in Blaze's hands. Blaze shot me a dead panned look, "Elton John over here thought it be good to serenade you... let me tell you this was against my will."

I chuckled at the Elton John remark but raised an eyebrow at Ryan, what did Blaze mean? Before I could question, Blaze started to strum the guitar grudgingly. I watched his blue eyes as he closed them and began to sing.

Baby you light up my world like nobody else, The way that you flip your hair gets me overwhelmed, But when you smile at the ground it ain't hard to tell, You don't know, Oh oh, You don't know you're beautiful,

Blaze stopped and shoved the guitar back to Ryan, "Happy? I sung your gay song!" Ryan smiled, "Extremely!!!" before he left practically prancing away. I chuckled, I bent down so I was Blaze's height, "You know he probably filmed that?"

Blaze's eye twitched, "I will kill him…"

I bit my lip, irritable Blaze was just too funny. I grabbed onto the back of the wheelchair and pushed him towards the table before taking a seat across from him. Blaze looked at me with a funny expression. "What?"

"My girlfriend's bloody breathtaking," he mumbled, his eyes gazed over me make my cheeks heat up. "Never pinned you as a romantic one Blaze."

Blaze wiggled his brows, "You from Tennessee? Because you're the only ten I see…" I smacked his arm, "And then you ruin it." He just laughed, "I hope… um everything is alright?" he gestured to the candles flickering and the really delicious pasta in front of me.

"It's perfect," I squeezed his hand in reassurance, who knew the selfish, cocky player could be nervous; he bit his lip before digging into his pasta. I watched Blaze, we had come so far from fighting and disagreeing to him being my rock. If I had a chance to redo things, I wouldn't change anything, because I met Blaze this way and fell in love with him this way.

We ate in silence, i could feel Blaze's eyes on me when I finished. "Can you believe it, graduating within two weeks?" I smiled at my plate, everything changes when you leave high school – especially your romantic life. I didn't want to lose Blaze.

"Its gone so fast, I don't want to move…"

Blaze laughed, his eyes crinkled when he did, "Get any acceptance letters yet?"

I nodded, "Harvard..." Blaze eyes widened, he nearly knocked the whole table over in excitement. He wheeled himself over and pulled me into his lap, "Congratulations beautiful! Wow my girlfriend's beautiful and smart," his arms snaked around my waist, I leaned back into him.

"Thank you, what about you?"

"Uhh... that's what I needed to talk to you about Mace..." my head spun so fast I'm pretty sure I got whiplash. I watched hesitantly as Blaze's eyes avoided mine, "I've ummm... a while back I signed up for the army reserve, and I've actually been offered to start my training when I finish school..."

"Blaze... I understand the country needs you and I know I'm being selfish but... I need you..." my voice cracked, Blaze pulled me into him, "I know Macy but were both going with our careers, and this is the path I've chosen. You know I'll visit you whenever I can!"

I snuggled my head into the crook of his neck, "Does that mean you're going to get a buzz cut?" I giggled at the thought of Blaze's hair being shaved off, Blaze's eyes widened before he groaned, "Oh well, it'll bring out my sexy ears..." he teased before kissing my nose.

"I love you."

Blaze chuckled, "I'm pretty irresistible aren't i?" I slapped his shoulder. "I love you Macy Hawthorne." He placed his lips on mine, I moved in sync with his. I smiled as he tried to nibble my lip for entrance, I just kept my mouth firmly shut.

"Mace!" I heard Blaze mumble against my lips, I let out a laugh allowing him entrance; our tongues collided as he fought dominance. This sweet kiss had turn into a full on snog fess of lust. I shivered in pleasure as he ran his hands down my back, my hands had found their way into his hair, tangling themselves.

I bit back a groan as Blaze kissed down my jaw to my neck, "Blaze..." I muttered breathlessly.

"Mhmm?"

"I...I... I want you to make love to me..."

Blaze pulled away, his eyes widened, "Macy..."

I nodded, "No I'm sure Blaze, I want my first time to be with the person I love, and you're the one I love."

"Now?"

"No better time than the present," my finger traced down the side of his face, Blaze's eyes watched me warily, "There's no hurry Mace."

"Blaze..."

"But were in a hospital..." Blaze glanced around.

I grinned, "So?"

Blaze just chuckled, "Classy Macy, your first time in a hospital. Not really a special moment to keep is it?"

I leaned my forehead against his, "If it's with you, no matter where we are then it will always be a special moment to me."

Blaze placed a soft kiss on my lip, "Some people will just say anything to get people into bed," he laughed, resulting in me slapping his arm. I let out a laugh as Blaze mocked a hurt face and began to wheel his wheelchair towards the elevator, this moment couldn't be even more perfect.

Graduation Day - Chapter 23

Macy's P.O.V

"Today's the day!" my father announced proudly as he clamped his hands down on my shoulders. I glanced at my mum who was bawling her eyes out, for god's sake the graduation ceremony hasn't even started. I glanced down at Felicity who was dressed up in a lime green dress and pigged tails, she shot me a sly grin, "When you go to college, I get ALL your stuff!"

I raised my brow at her, even though she annoys me to death – I was going to miss her. In about 2-3 weeks' time I was moving into Harvard Campus, much to my mother's protest I insisted on getting a place up there with Selena who had gotten into Harvard too.

"They grow up so quickly!" my mother let out a howl before she proceeded to cry onto my father's shirt. I laughed as dad mumbled something about her ruining his favourite shirt. "Dad, I'm just going to see Chloe – I'll see you after the ceremony!" my dad gave me a brisk nod as he tried to detached mum.

I walked past the buzzing crowds of relatives of my classmates, I could spot a few familiar people who wore their black graduation caps. I made my way to the bubbling blonde who was animatedly talking to Luke, I chuckled – their relationship was so bipolar. One minute they would fight, Chloe would come crying to me and then the next minute Luke and her would be going at it like sex-crazed animals.

I pulled Chloe into a hug as she squealed into my ear, "Can you believe were graduating!" I peeked around her shoulder to see Luke roll his eyes playfully at Chloe. "Luke where you planning to go after this?" I asked, I didn't really Luke that well – but he really does make Chloe happy.

Luke ran his fingers through his blonde hair, his graduation cap tucked under his arm, "Oxford, surprised I got accepted though," he smiled at me as he wrapped his arms around Chloe. "Wow, congratulations!"

Chloe stuck her lower lip out, "You're all leaving me! And I'm going to be here at the local community college all by myself," she complained. Luke squeezed her shoulders, "You know you can come visit us."

"And there will be plenty more relationships for you to meddle with in college!" Luke and I both cracked up before Chloe threw a hard punch at my arm. "Ow!" I yelped. Chloe smirk grew wider, "You deserved it!"

I jumped in surprise when two arms wrapped around my waist, a deep voice whispered into my eear causing me to shiver, "Hello beautiful."

"Blaze!" his blue eyes were starring right into mine.

"I have surprise for you after the ceremony!"

"More surprises?"

Blaze just laughed as he nodded, Ryan joined the conversation with his hands on his hips, "You're a spoilt princess!"

I pegged Ryan in the arm, "I'm a lucky girl," before placing a kiss on Blaze lips.

"AHH MY EYES!" Luke and Chloe shrieked.

"Hypocrites! You two go at it no matter who's in the room!" Blaze protested.

"I blame it on hormones..." Chloe stated as she snuggled into Luke's side.

The three of us shook our heads at the bipolar couple. "Please take your seats as the ceremony is about to start." Principle William's voice boomed over the loud speaker. I grabbed Ryan's hand since we had to sit in alphabetical order, he would be right next to me.

Blaze shot me his breath taking smile, it was still hard to believe he was mine, "Meet on you on the other side."

"I'll be the one in graduation robe."

"Along with the whole grade."

"Touché," I shot him a wink before Ryan pulled me to my seat.

"Baby you did it!" my mother smoothed me in a big a hug as soon as the ceremony had finished, I awkwardly patted her on the back, "Mum..."

"I'm so proud!"

"Mum... you're suffocating me!"

"Oh, sorry about that sweetie," mum released me before smoothing down her crumpled clothes. Dad chuckled, "Go have fun with your friends, but remember be home for dinner, the whole family's coming over."

I placed a kiss on his cheek, "Thanks Dad."

I gave them all a wave as I jogged up to the gang who were waiting for me. "Sorry, mum got a bit emotional!"

Selena laughed, "Don't worry; my brother wouldn't let me go!"

"Ready?" Chloe gripped my hand tightly, as I glanced around at as all huddle in a circle in the parking lot, grinning like idiots – we were truly happy. We had overcome every little drama in high school, made unlikely decisions, fallen in love and finally graduated. But this wasn't the end, it was just the beginning.

"Ready," I answered.

"1... 2... 3!"

I watched in awe as our graduation caps flew up into the sky before quickly returning to the ground. Luke chuckled, "Wasn't quite like the movies."

I wrapped my arms around Blaze's waist, "But it was perfect."

Ryan slung his arm around Blaze and me causing us to separate, "Now let's party!"

"But here's my number so call me maybe!" Ryan sung out of tune as he took another swig of his beer. I leaned into Blaze's chest as we watched everyone dancing in the middle of Ryan's basement.

I laughed, "Its only 3pm, and he's drunk..."

"And a terrible singer!" Blaze added.

"Agreed."

"Want to go somewhere quiet?" Blaze stood up offering his hand to me, I accepted it as he pulled me up from the floor, "Lead the way." With hands held clamped tight together I followed Blaze as we made our way out of Ryan's basement and on to his balcony.

"So Macy about that surprise…" Blaze was leaning over the railing glancing at the amazing view Ryan's house had of the ocean. I looked up at him in confusion, "Wh-what is it?" curiosity was eating me up.

Blaze turned to look at me before pulling out a rectangular shaped present out of his jacket. "I got you a graduation present…" My eyes widened before I slapped him on the shoulder, "I thought we said no presents!"

"I wanted to surprise you!" Blaze raised his hands up in alarm, I laughed before giving him a bone crushing hug, "You idiot, I got you a present too…"

I felt his chin gently rest on my head, "You goof, so much for no presents." I pulled out the small package in my dress pocket and shoved it towards him, "There you go!" in return I got the rectangular present in my hands.

Without waiting I unwrapped the wrapping paper to see a wooden frame with a picture of Blaze and me at Valentine's Day dance, I bit my lip – the picture was beautiful. I was wrapped up in Blaze's arm, and I seem to be beaming at him like an idiot. "Macy…"

My head shot up to see Blaze had opened his present, I shot him a cheesy grin. It was hard to decide what to get him, I asked Ryan – but he gave me a completely disturbing idea… so I thought of something that he would be able to take to the army with him.

Blaze slipped the tag and silver chain over his head, "Did you like the inscription?" I questioned.

"There's a date…" Blaze face flashed with confusion.

"Yes silly, the date… where… we umm…"

"Where we what?"

"You know…"

"Did the dirty crime in the school shed?" Blaze winked at me sending me blushing red before punching him in the arm, "AHH HELP ABUSIVE RELATIONSHIP!" (IS NO JOKE AND SHOULD BE SERIOUSLY TAKEN UNLESS YOUR A PERVERT LIKE BLAZE) Blaze hollered as he gripped his arm in agony.

"Kissed…"

Blaze's mouth formed on 'O' before he quickly understood and pulled me into a hug, "I love it Mace, I really do!" I wrapped my arms around his waist, "I like your present too, can't believe you got a picture from that day!"

"Well it was pretty easy since Chloe had taken so many photos!" Blaze chuckled causing his whole body to shake, I soon joined in laughing. "You know I'm going to miss you so much Blaze… I leave in 2 weeks, and you a day after that…"

"I know…"

"I'll only see you a few times a year if I'm lucky…" I could feel tears brimming at my eyes, how could I stand here and let someone I love go.

Blaze tipped my chin up, "Macy, you don't have to wait for me. I'm not going to make you wait because who knows when I return you might have moved on. So let's not worry about then, let's just enjoy now."

I snuggled back into his hug; "Blaze…" the sound was muffled by his shirt.

"Yeah?"

"For the record, I'll wait."

"So will I princess, so will i…"

It felt so perfect just right there in each other's arms, but I knew it wouldn't last forever but I've excepted we have to go our separate ways as a part of our future.

"YO! Guys wanna here a wise quote!" Ryan shoved the sliding doors open interrupting my thoughts. I removed my head from Blaze's chest, "What?" answering the drunk Ryan who was swaying dangerously. "If life was a garden…. Don't be a hoe! Get it hoe! AH HOE! I'm hilarious!" Ryan was laughing to himself while Blaze laughing at Ryan's lame quote.

Shaking my head, I let out a laugh…I've learnt a lot from this, I've meet some amazing people and I've lost some people I thought I love. I've learnt that bad things are always going to happen in life. People will hurt you, but you can't use that as an excuse to hurt someone back. I guess I'm trying to say, the best REVENGE, is letting go of the past and moving on.

Coming Home - Epilogue

NO SEQUELS

- thank you for supporting this story, all of you -

EPILOGUE

5 years later

"Coming through! Excuse me! Would you move? Pregnant lady coming through!" a loud voice shouted as they tried to maneuver their way through the busy airport. It was quite a sight seeing my very pregnant best friend waddle towards me with her exhausted looking husband in toll.

Ryan chuckled beside me before leaning towards my ear, "Does she always do that?" Ryan had just returned a few days ago from overseas where he had been studying abroad. It was so good to have the old gang back. I chuckled before replying, "It's so no one mistakes her as fat..."

Ryan snorted, "Oh she hasn't changed at all..." I nodded in agreement before walking towards a frustrated Chloe as she managed to squeeze in between a backpacking couple. "Chloe!" her lips curled into a smile before she pulled me into an awkward side hug. A few seconds later another body had wrapped themselves around us, no doubt it was Ryan himself.

I looked across Chloe shoulders to see Luke dragging Chloe's numerous bags, how he's managed to stay with her for 5 years is a mystery to me. "You guys seriously started the group hug without me?" a new voice spoke causing us to detach to see a woman with a blonde bob. I gasp as Chloe jumped on Selena, "You look so different!"

As soon as we graduated Selena had gotten a scholarship into a performing arts school. We kept in touch through text and emails but this was the first time I've seen her in 5 years. "I thought you weren't going to make it?" I asked as I gave Selena a gentle hug, she grasped my shoulders firmly, "There was no way I was going to my best friends special day."

I could feel my cheeks turn red as I tightened my scarf around my neck, "It's not that special…" Chloe just rolled her eyes, "Nonsense, it's the day Blaze is coming back from the army!" That's when reality hit me, it had been 5 years since Blaze was shipped off to the army, it was hard to have contact with him – with only the exception of monthly letters.

What if something had happened to him? You see soldiers come back from war, and their never the same. I shook the thoughts away, I'm just being selfish – all I should want is for him to be safe in my arms. "Macy!" Ryan nudged me in the sides causing me to break out of my thoughts, "Daydreaming of Blaze?" he raised a brow suggestively.

I slapped his shoulder, "No, you dirty pervert. I was just thinking… if he's the same guy I fell in love with."

Ryan rested his arm around my shoulder, "Macy you're over thinking this, you and Blaze care deeply about each other and nothings ever going change that. Sure he may look different or do little things differently but he will always love you. Come on; be happy, he's finally coming home forever." I glanced up at Ryan; tears were already blurring my vision.

"Thank you Ryan," I muttered before I buried my face in the crook of his neck, Ryan was right – I should focus on what's important here, Blaze. "FLIGHT S062J is now landing at Gate 5," the intercom managed to choke out the announcement before cutting off. "That's Blaze's flight!" I announced to my best friends as I followed the overhead signs to Gate 5.

'''

It felt like forever, watching other families embrace their loved ones, watching people slowly emerge from the plane. I was frantically looking from person to person, afraid I had miss one second to see him. That's when a dark head caught my eyes; I felt my heart fasten as I took in his appearance. His once shaggy hair had been cut short, his eyes still the same color of blue and not to mention that notorious smirk.

He had bulked up since 5 years ago, compared to now – he was a scrawny little boy back then. I could feel my legs automatically walking towards him; I couldn't help notice the small scar on the side of his forehead, something that hadn't been there originally.

"Macy..." as he mumbled my name I was already in his arms. My legs were wrapped around his waist as my arms encircled his neck. I let out a big sob that I had been holding in since I had first seen him step out of the airplane.

"I've missed you so much..." I murmured into his collarbone.

"Macy... Macy can't breathe!" Blaze choked out as I realized I had been hugging him too tightly. I let out a nervous laugh as I untangled myself from him. "Sorry," I muttered shyly as soon as my feet hit the ground.

I felt warm hands graze my cheek before my head was tilted towards Blaze; he still managed to be a head taller than me! "Macy Hawthorne, I never thought I'd ever be saying this, but here I am. Our senior year was one of kind and to be honest I thought you were just going to forget me once you got over Aaron. But you didn't, and I certainly didn't forget you. You've become my best friend who happens to be my girlfriend. I would sit through all the reruns of Oprah and The Notebook for you. God this sounds so god damn cheesy, but Macy Hawthorne I love you and will you do me the honor of becoming my wife?"

"You're suppose to kneel, you idiot!" a voice shouted from the crowd that had now formed. No doubt that was Ryan's words of wisdom. Blaze's words were clouding my mind, Ryan was right – he may have changed appearance and other things but he still loved me. I felt cold tears splashing down my cheeks.

"Yes..." I whispered before the crowd exploded into applause and congratulations but I didn't care, all that matter was that I was in Blaze's arms and he was safe. I slowly pulled away, "That scar... where did you get it?" my mind was coming up with all these terrifying scenarios when Blaze interrupted me, "I fell over in one of the trenches..." I let out a snort; I had been worried for nothing.

"Congratulations!" Selena shouted in my ear as she pulled Blaze and me in for a hug.

"It's funny we've grown up so much from senior year... I never thought this could all happen," Ryan stated as he flashed me cheeky smile.

"To think were all grown up, our adventures will be over!" Chloe let out a loud wail before burying herself in Luke's side.

Luke just shook his head at his wife, "Well honey, it's not over till the fat lady sings..."

"Warm up your vocal chords Chloe!" Ryan said causing all of us to burst out laughing except for Chloe who had already taken to hitting Ryan with her handbag.

"God damn it lady! What do you put in there a brick?" The rest of us watched their childish bickering, we may have grown up but were still young at heart. I guess things really do turn out for the best, they may not seem at the exact moment but in the future you'll get your happily ever after.

The End

www.ingramcontent.com/pod-product-compliance
Lightning Source LLC
Chambersburg PA
CBHW072209070526
44585CB00015B/1253